Raising Kids Right in a World Gone Wrong

Raising Kids Right in a World Gone Wrong

DUANE & LEEANN RAWLINS

Emerald Books

P.O. Box 635
Lynnwood, Washington 98046

RAISING KIDS RIGHT IN A WORLD GONE WRONG

Dedication

*W*ith love to our six children: Mark Rawlins, Matthew Rawlins, Mindy Berry, and Mark, Lonnie, and Robert Smucker, who lovingly put up with our parenting. All six are truly a blessing to us from the Lord.

Acknowledgments

*T*hanks to who helped us — our editors: Geoff and Janet Benge, Mary Owens, and Deborah Cady; special thanks to Matt Rawlins for Chapter Two; Ray Maul, who helped with computer work, and to everyone who gave us encouragement and support for this book.

Foreword

*I*t has been our privilege to know Duane and LeeAnn for many years. Both Duane and LeeAnn bring to their marriage a tried-and-true set of family principles, and their lives and children bear witness to the genuineness of their faith.

It has been refreshing to see how two people from differing backgrounds and denominations (LeeAnn from a strong Mennonite farming family; Duane from an educator's background) can be so united in Christ-centered goals for families.

Duane is the kind of man who will stop during a conversation at breakfast or lunch and say, "Let's pray about this." When discussing a complicated business venture, he will ask, "How can this glorify God?" By his example, he encourages accountability to the Lordship of Jesus Christ in our dealings.

LeeAnn is the kind of woman who takes the pain of losing family members and turns it into compassion for others who are going through the same thing. We met a woman at a conference just last week who'd "just happened" to sit next to LeeAnn on a plane, and LeeAnn had counseled her and prayed with her. The woman said LeeAnn had pointed her to

Christ when she was at a desperate place in her life, contemplating suicide. This is just a "normal" thing for both of them to do—to reach out to anyone near them with love.

Duane and LeeAnn's message in this book comes out of hearts that beat as one—that families can truly be lights in this world, and that it is possible to lead our families in this complex and difficult world to be true disciples of Jesus Christ. Theirs is not a dull, harsh religion. There's a lot of laughter and joy in their families, and they are "real people." But they've caught onto a great secret: If Jesus Christ is Lord of us as individuals, and Lord of our families, we have real purpose, real joy...

...Something *very right* in a world gone wrong!

Bill and Nancie Carmichael
Founding Co-Publishers of Good Family Magazines
Christian Parenting Today, Virtue, Parents of Teenagers

Table of Contents

Introduction
A World Gone Wrong

*A*lthough not a fan of Bob Dylan, I was recently drawn to one of his albums, *World Gone Wrong*. How descriptive is that title. It pictures so succinctly how most people see the world today—a world gone wrong.

As I write this introduction, the brutality of Bosnia and the indescribable carnage of Rwanda along with the usual fare of violence, crime and corruption fill our news reports. Our reaction to all of this is often fear, frustration and anger followed by a sense of despair, hopelessness and a lot of sadness.

I'm often tempted to despair when I see horrendous things going on in the world. Then I recall the words of the old spiritual: "He's got the whole world in His hands." Despite what we think and feel about the state of the world, God holds it in His hands. He is in control.

I have difficulty understanding why many of the things that happen in this world happen. I cannot see God's big picture to gain the perspective that I need to fully guide my comprehension. So I trust that

He is in control and is moving the world along a path He has mapped out for it.

Faced with the current state of the world, I see a disturbing paradox as I look around the Church today. The more needy the world becomes, the less Christians seem to become involved in it. Christians seem to think that being a Christian is more comfortable when they withdraw as much as possible from the world and cluster themselves together. They form the spiritual equivalent of the "gated communities" that are so popular in many cities today.

Unfortunately for Christians, gated communities and the commands of Jesus stand at odds. Jesus' focus was never on the comfort, safety and security of living behind the gate. Rather, His eyes were always on the needs of those who dwelled beyond the gate— the people who needed His touch, the people to whom He went, the people He commands Christians to go to today.

Though the Bible tells us not to love the world, we must remember that we are still in it, and are commanded to love others. Perhaps the reason the world has gone wrong is that Christians have forgotten that they are called to be the dispensers of God's great love for all people. Perhaps Christians have become more interested in themselves than in disbursing God's grace and love. Perhaps God is grieved by our actions. While we eagerly await His second coming to be plucked from this wretched world, perhaps we are actually delaying its arrival by our inaction.

Perhaps if we were to again involve ourselves in taking Christ's message to all mankind, we could turn the world around, back from the brink of social, moral, economic, ecological and spiritual collapse. Perhaps we could change the world to reflect the values and character of the God who made it.

Perhaps.

Today, God is looking for Christians with a sense of "perhaps" in their hearts. He wants a new generation of world-changers who will turn the world upside down with the gospel message, as did the early disciples. During the 1960s and 1970s, such people would have been referred to as radicals. God is looking for a new generation of radicals who are willing to serve Him 100 percent.

In the Church today, we have wrongfully developed a certain class structure where the truly godly people work as "full-time servants of God," and those who work outside the Church aren't considered to be doing anything Christian unless they are witnessing. We desperately need to eliminate the idea of work as being either secular or sacred.

Far too often we think that being Christian consists of going to church, worshiping, reading our Bibles, witnessing and living moral lives. Rarely does it enter our minds that being a good Christian may have much more to do with the world of art, literature, politics, service, parenting, fishing and all of those things that we do for forty, fifty or sixty hours a week.

The radical young people God seeks are those who know their faith should affect every level and area of their life. Many of them will probably serve God in "full-time" positions, but many will not. Regardless of how or where they serve, they all realize they are to serve God in everything they do. Everywhere they go, in every situation they face, to every person they encounter, they are bearers of the Gospel. They are called to change the world by declaring God's truth and ministering His love to every level of every society on earth.

Where does God find these people? If we are Christian parents, He looks to our children. Radical Christians are nurtured and raised by parents who instill in their children the importance of loving God and living their lives for Him.

In our broken-down world, it's not easy raising radical Christian kids. Many things, often sinful things, vie for their attention. The spirits of the age—materialism, humanism, self-centeredness, promiscuity and sexual infidelity—look to seduce the unwary at every turn. Despite these spirits, raising radical Christian children today is not impossible.

Together, LeeAnn and I have raised two very different families. She and her first husband, Willard, raised three boys on their farm in Oregon. They lived on the same farm all their married lives and attended the same close-knit Mennonite church. Since I was busy with my career as an educator and a real estate agent, my first wife, Betty, and I moved around a lot. Despite the numerous moves, my daughter and two sons learned to adapt to new situations and make friends at the various churches we attended.

On the outside, there was not a lot in common in the way we raised our children. Yet when people meet our blended family, they often comment on how similar our children are. Except for my oldest son, Mark, who died several years ago of cancer, each is happily married to a partner he or she chose for life. They all lead active Christian lives and have been involved with their spouses in some form of missionary service. And all are actively involved in making the world they live in a better place for themselves, their families and their communities. Between us, my wife and I raised a pastor, a farm manager, a choir director, a doctor and a manufacturer.

Our children were raised in different environments by different parents, yet they all carry the same basic set of values into their adult lives. Each is serving the Lord in his or her unique way, and God is using each to touch the lives of the next generation.

During the eight years that LeeAnn and I have been married, many people have asked us the secret of raising happy, well-adjusted kids who want to wholeheartedly serve the Lord. When we began to compare notes, we discovered that although the external conditions under which we raised our families differed, we followed the same essential course. That doesn't mean we (or our respective spouses) were totally consistent or without our share of frustrations and setbacks. But at the heart of our families, we operated from the same basic understandings.

As we shared these perceptions with groups of parents around the world, we decided it was time to synthesize them into book form.

The temptation in a book whose focus is to challenge parents to challenge their children to live wholeheartedly for the Lord is to tell everything we learned about child-rearing along the way. That's not an easy temptation to resist, but to the best of our abilities, we have tried to confine our comments to those areas directly related to nurturing children's spiritual lives so that the children might grow up to become truly radical Christians. And while this book is not meant to be exhaustive, we know from experience that these principles do work.

This book is written humbly in the hope that it will stir other parents to raise radical children for the kingdom of God. Our prayer is that you will take these principles and apply them in your family, that together we may raise a generation of radical Christians who will truly fix our world gone wrong by the power of the Gospel.

God's Mandate to Christian Parents

It is easier for a father to have children than for children to have a real father.
Pope John XXIIL

CHAPTER ONE

*H*ow true are Pope John's words! It is easier to go through the biological steps of producing a child than to parent that child successfully to adulthood. Listening to the concerns and challenges that face our children and their spouses as they raise our grandchildren, LeeAnn and I have become aware that the task of parenting children to adulthood with a vibrant, dynamic faith and world-changing goals is harder than ever. But it is not impossible.

No, times aren't easy. But tough times build character. The apostle Paul said, "But where sin increased, grace increased all the more" (Romans 5:20). And in 1 Peter 1:7, Peter says: "These [trials] have come so that your faith...may be proved genuine and may result in praise, glory and honor when Jesus Christ is revealed."

While lecturing in various countries around the world, I've seen the truth of these words. Despite the compromising times in which we live, I am constantly impressed with the strong faith and solid character of the young people who talk to LeeAnn and me. These witnesses have committed their lives to discipleship and to having an impact on the world around them with the Gospel.

God is interested in speaking to and through this generation, and we are the primary people who can promote the right conditions within our homes to make this possible. Parenting is not easy by today's standards, but as parents, we have been given a Christian mandate by which to raise godly children.

Leading Our Families

> *Now fear the Lord and serve him with all faithfulness.... But if serving the Lord seems undesirable to you, then choose for yourselves this day whom you will serve....But as for me and my household, we will serve the Lord.* — Joshua 24:14-15

I can imagine Joshua standing atop a hill delivering this challenge to the children of Israel. Joshua recounted all the past things God had done for them and then gave them a choice: Whom were they going to serve? But he didn't wait for their reply before announcing to the assembled throng that regardless of their choice, he and his family were going to serve God.

Joshua was a true family leader. He didn't wait to see what the prevailing social or political climate was before making a decision as to what he and his family would do. Rather, he was pro-active. He personally was going to serve the Lord, and he was going to lead his family in doing the same.

We need Joshua's attitude today. We must be pro-active if our children are to develop into everything God wants them to be. We can't afford to take a back seat to worldly influences, including our children's non-Christian friends and other nonbelievers they meet. Our families need clear direction to know where they are headed.

In the March 28, 1994, issue of *Time,* former President George Bush said, "I firmly believe that the biggest danger to us is the disintegration of the American family." This would have sounded trite and simplistic ten years ago, but today the same thought is echoed everywhere. Liberals and conservatives, black and white, rich and poor are all coming to the same conclusion. Everywhere we turn, people are waking up to the fact that nations are made up of families, not individuals. The family is the backbone of our great nation, and without strong families we are sunk. Today, we desperately need families who will make the same pledge that Joshua made.

God made families to be the primary unit within which we learn values, practice social skills and grow in our faith. God has given parents the awesome task of leading these families. More than ever, we need to accept the challenge that role offers.

Besides having talked to many dedicated Christian young people, I have talked to many who are trying to find a way through the tangled web of their supposed Christian upbringing. Their parents' imposing on them things they were unwilling or unable to live out in their own lives has left them with scars of bitterness, confusion, rebellion and self-loathing. But Joshua's injunction was, "As for me and my house." That's the order in which things should be done in our families.

We will never get our children to do anything that we ourselves are unwilling to do. Thus, the challenge to parents is to be all God intends for us to be. If we do this, our lives will affect our children in a life-changing way. We cannot lead from an armchair. By definition, to "lead" means to be out in front, to trail-blaze, to show the way, to set the pace for those who come behind. As parents, we are to take our position of leadership at the head of our family. When we lead by positive example, the rest of our family can follow.

While God has given us this model, we must remember there's a difference between being authoritarian and being authoritative.

An *authoritarian parent* makes arbitrary, inflexible rules that leave no room for negotiation. This parent's attitude is, "I am the boss around here, so we'll do things my way." This parent turns decisions into confrontations, not compromises. This parent says, "Do it because I say so," not, "Do it because God says so."

Floyd McClung, Jr., compares parenting styles using the terms *dominating* or *suffocating* vs. *godly* (fathers in the Lord). Following are some comparisons he uses to differentiate these two approaches:

- Emphasizing the rights of leaders vs. emphasizing the responsibilities of leaders.

- Seeking to control people's actions vs. encouraging people to be dependent on God.

- Using rules to control people and forcing them to conform to a mold vs. providing an atmosphere of trust and grace to encourage spiritual growth.

McClung stresses that godly fathers know the character of the heavenly Father, and follow His direction in the way they work with their children.

The basic problem with authoritarian parents is that they believe they should be obeyed because of what they say, whereas the biblical model is for parents to be obeyed because of what they do. God expects us to obey Him, not because of anything He says, but because of all the ways He demonstrates to us that He loves us and cares for us. He models the correct attitudes we are to show our children. Our obedience is the same as if God demanded it of us, but our motive for obeying is rooted in love and respect, not in fear and hatred. God has given us authority to promote and to encourage those under us, not to force them to do our bidding.

Authoritative parents, on the other hand, are sensitive to their children's needs. Warmth and understanding are at the heart of the relationship between parent and child, resulting in good communication among family members. Reason is present in the relationship, developing trust between parent and child. This type family has structure and age-appropriate rules that make sense. Instructions are clear and simple, and the consequences for wrongdoing are clearly spelled out well before problems arise. Dealings within the authoritative family are carried out in a spirit of love, with the goal always that of bringing change, not condemnation.

The first obligation God requires of us as Christian parents is to lead our families, not in an authoritarian way, but in an atmosphere of love and respect that leads to the development of confidence and trust in our children's lives.

We need to lead our families as tenderly as God leads us. And nowhere is this tenderness better expressed than in Isaiah 40:11: "He tends his flock like a shepherd: He gathers the lambs in his arms and carries them close to his heart; he gently leads those that have young."

If the all-knowing, all-wise God is that gentle with us, we who are fallible and prone to misjudge situations need to be even gentler as we lead our families.

Teaching and Training

Train a child in the way he should go, and when he is old he will not turn from it.
— Proverbs 22:6

If you're like me, when you're trying to construct something or to get a new appliance to work, you probably take several problem-solving approaches before giving in and reading the instruction manual. Usually we turn to the manual as a last resort. Of course, if we wait too long and do irreparable damage to our blender or toaster or the thing we're building, we can replace it.

But not so with our children. If we irreparably damage our children while raising them, we and our children must live with the consequences all the days of our lives.

Our carefree attitude to getting an appliance to work right or building a dog house is not the proper approach to raising children. Rather, God's instruction manual for families—the Bible—should be where we turn first, not after the fact. In it is found God's blueprint for the family. If we study it well, we can avoid a lot of unnecessary damage in our lives and in our children's lives.

The Bible's wisdom about family relationships goes far beyond any other resource. As effective parents, we need to become effective men and women in accordance with the Word of God. We need to learn from the Bible on a daily basis, recording as we go the wisdom the Lord reveals to us. His revelations will enable us to mold our children step by step into the people God created them to be. In the process, we are able to fulfill another responsibility God gives us as parents: training our children.

In exercising our responsibility, it is important for us to know exactly what is meant by God's instructions. *Training* is defined as "to mold the character, instruct by exercise, drill; to make obedient to orders; to put or point in an exact direction; to prepare for a contest." Training implies showing by example how and why we do things.

Training our children requires more than taking them to church every Sunday just because we think it is good for them. Training requires more than just telling them that there is a God and that He loves them. It requires our taking them to church because we are convinced in our hearts that church is where we should be each Sunday to worship and commune with the Lord. It requires our demonstrating through our actions toward our children that there is a God and that He loves us. Such actions influence our children far beyond anything we can say. Our actions speak louder than our words.

Each child is a unique individual, and taking that uniqueness into account when training our children is important. When it comes to discipline, the old adage, "The punishment must fit the crime," is only partly true; it must also fit the one who committed the offense. And it must be administered with the goal of bringing understanding to the child and restoring his or her relationship with the parents. To expect punishment in itself to provide anything but negative results is a tragic mistake. Punishment without a firm foundation of unconditional love and proper training only creates a poor relationship between parents and child. Unfortunately, in both Christian and non-Christian homes, negative punishment is all too common a form of discipline.

As we train our children, they learn to love, trust and obey us. As the years go by, these attributes are eventually transferred to their relationship with God.

Nurturing and Encouraging

Fathers, do not embitter your children, or they will become discouraged.—Colossians 3:21

Research on developing self-esteem suggests that it takes ten "atta-boys" to make up for one put-down. That's a sobering finding to keep in mind the next time we feel tempted to tell our child that he or she is lazy, careless or stupid.

Whether we like it or not, the way other people view us has a major impact on what we say, how we think, how we feel and how we act. So, too, for our children. If we constantly berate and criticize them, and convince them they're not capable people, most likely they will conform to our low expectations.

Cognizant of this fact, Paul, in the course of writing to the Colossians, reminded fathers of their responsibility to nurture and encourage their children so they don't become embittered. Paul knew how easy it was for parents—especially fathers—to vent their frustrations on their children. The end result is hurt for the child, which can lead to alienation from the parent and even to the severing of the parent-child relationship. The ultimate consequence is often hurt for all involved.

Children respond to encouragement, not discouragement. Pleasant words, according to Proverbs 16:24 (Amplified), "are as a honeycomb, sweet to the mind and healing to the body." Our children are nourished by our words as well as by our physical attention. Encouragement shows them honor and respect, important ingredients in every healthy relationship. Without respect, deep relationships cannot endure.

Psychologists have found that to maintain emotional and physical health, adults need eight to ten meaningful touches every day. How much more so do our children! The smallest act of touching can be a vehicle to communicate love and personal acceptance. Reach out and touch your children. Touching is important to their well-being.

Unfortunately, today's society has developed a certain paranoia about touching others. We fear that our touch will be wrongly interpreted as having some covert or perverse purpose. This atmosphere affects even Christian families. Instead of maintaining healthy physical contact by which affection toward family members can be shared, fathers in particular pull away from their daughters or sons, especially as the children approach and enter adolescence. Somehow men feel it is inappropriate to hold or to hug their children. But nothing is further from the truth. Our children, even in adolescence, need the encouraging, loving and affirming touch of their parents. Touching is a tangible expression of the parents' love for their children.

LeeAnn and I have spent hour after hour listening to young men and women pour out their hearts as they shared deep hurts they experienced because their parents, especially their fathers, failed to show them love and affection in an appropriate physical way. Young people in their twenties sobbed bitterly because they had never experienced a hug from their father or mother. Often this occurs not because of a deliberate choice by the parent, but because the parent was unable or unwilling to express his or her love for the child through an understandable medium. In many cases, this inaction stemmed from a lack in the parent's own upbringing.

Several years ago, I was teaching at a Youth With A Mission (YWAM) training school. A young man who had recently converted from atheism to Christianity approached me after class to ask a question. As I answered his query, I placed my hand on his shoulder, as I often do with people I talk to. I thought nothing of it.

About a year later, the young man came back to YWAM. One day, he called me aside and asked if I remembered putting my hand on his shoulder during our conversation. Then he looked me in the eyes and said, "You will never know how much that meant to me. I was so unfamiliar with being touched that it blew me away! It changed my life."

Such a simple thing. Touching his shoulder took only a couple of seconds, but the effects of the touch will last that young man a lifetime.

As parents, we must let our children know how we feel toward them. We may never realize how much a special time set aside or a special touch will show our love for them.

At a recent Sunday evening church service, I noticed a small boy lying with his head resting on his father's knee. The father was gently stroking the boy's hair. I could not help but watch as the little boy smiled and gently dropped off to sleep. The father was sending a strong message of love and support as his hand stroked the boy's head. Tears began to fill my eyes as I viewed this warm expression of love being given and received without any verbal expression whatsoever.

Nurturing and encouraging our children are part of God's mandate to parents. We must diligently use the appropriate means to discharge this responsibility and raise emotionally healthy, well-balanced children who are aware that they are loved, honored and respected.

Providing Materially

> *After all, children should not have to save up for their parents, but parents for their children.* —2 Corinthians 12:14

God intended for parents to provide the material needs of their family. It is inappropriate for children to take on the burden of how the family is going to make it until the end of the month or where their next pair of shoes is going to come from. Being a parent means committing to our children's material welfare. Often this translates into making decisions based on their needs rather than our own.

LeeAnn and I can both look back on times in our first marriages when we spent money that was not "spare cash" to help our children with something that would be of lasting value to them. Raising our family on modest incomes forced us to create very tight, no-frills budgets. When one month's money was gone, we waited until the following month for additional funds. A set of encyclopedias to provide research material for our children's schooling was paid for monthly over a two-year period.

Of course, providing for our children needs balance. While we don't want to unduly burden them with the responsibilities of the family's day-to-day existence, neither do we want to make things too easy for them. Coddling can make them self-centered and selfish. We should expect our children to undertake a few chores around the house to earn their weekly allowance, rather than just handing them money each week regardless of their behavior. By working for their allowance, children learn that money is earned and needs to be used wisely.

When your child is old enough to start mowing the lawn or vacuuming the rug, we believe it is important to make these chores a regular part of the child's work duties. Wise parents will, for the first few times, show a child how to complete the task efficiently. Plenty of encouragement, instead of constant criticism, will not only get the lawn mowed or the rug vacuumed, but will also build character and teach your child responsibility.

Another important dimension to this whole aspect of material provision is trusting God with and for our material possessions. If we want to raise dynamic Christian children with a sense of mission to change the world by the power of the Gospel, we must teach them this concept by example. When there isn't enough money to make ends meet, do we gather our family together and commit the situation to the Lord? When an emergency arises, are our children aware that we trust God to provide the necessary means with which to deal with the emergency? What about when God blesses us with an abundance of money and material possessions? Do we gather the family together to ask the Lord whom He wants us to bless from the abundance He has provided for us?

We are stewards over all that God gives us. There is no greater principle we can teach our children about material possessions than this. Viewing money and material possessions from this perspective will guard our children against the onslaught of selfishness so rampant in our world today.

Overseeing Spiritual Development

LeeAnn relates how a number of years ago she was talking with one of her friends who was raising young children. LeeAnn related to this friend her excitement over a child in the church who had recently accepted Jesus into her life. The friend didn't share LeeAnn's enthusiasm. In fact, she was horrified that a child would be encouraged to do such a thing. "I think it's tragic," she said to LeeAnn. "Young children should be free to be who they are. They shouldn't have to endure Christian life until they get older."

Unfortunately, LeeAnn's friend was seeing Christianity from the wrong perspective. To her, living a Christian life was nothing more than drudgery. She believed a relationship with the Lord to be based on obligation, not love. To her, the longer that obligation was put off, the better.

Many Christians have a similar attitude about Christian life, and it is often passed on to their children. Here again, we Christian parents need to lead our families by example. We must keep a positive attitude about being a Christian and having a personal relationship with Jesus.

Our job is to oversee the spiritual development of our children. More than at any other time, children need spiritual guidance to find their way through the maze of ungodly activities vying for their attention. We need to provide them with positive images of what it means to be a Christian. We need to show them how right it is to have a daily relationship with God so they will be drawn to Him, not being repelled and taken captive by worldly enticements.

LeeAnn's friend made her job more difficult by her negative attitude. Raising well-balanced children who enjoy a vibrant relationship with the Lord is never an easy task. Her example was more likely to re pel her children from Christianity than to draw them closer into relationship with the Lord.

Overseeing our children's spiritual development is one of the most important responsibilities God gives to us as parents, one we can't afford to be in two minds about. It takes single-minded devotion to spiritually nurture our children.

When my oldest son, Mark, died of cancer several years ago, we were very concerned about the welfare of his four children, all under the age of eight. But since then, we have seen such devotion and single-mindedness in their mother, Lynne. She is willing to drop less important things to take her children to the library or to chauffeur them to various activities. She is always cheering them on, nurturing their giftings and spiritual growth. All her hard work has resulted in her children's excelling in school, both academically and socially. Her positive example helps build their character. As a single parent, she is doing her very best to nurture and encourage her children.

Laying a Firm Foundation

> *By the grace God has given me, I laid a foundation as an expert builder, and someone else is building on it. But each one should be careful how he builds. For no one can lay any foundation other than the one already laid, which is Jesus Christ.*
> —1 Corinthians 3:10-11

As parents, our job is to lay a solid foundation in the lives of our children. This includes making sure our children are emotionally well-balanced, intellectually astute, physically healthy, spiritually attuned to the Gospel and enjoying a personal relationship with the Lord. It also means raising our children to have a firm and deep-rooted character that is nurtured by the principles found in God's Word.

Like Paul, we are to lay the foundation, but it is the job of others—in this case, our children—to build on that foundation. We can help the building process by offering advice and guidance, but it's not our job to do the building. Our children are responsible for what they make of themselves. They must set their own goals for what they want to become as adults. Our hope is that by our laying a firm foundation, our children can discern the biblical pattern for building on that foundation.

A few years ago, a young man came to the Salem YWAM training center. Despite his poor foundation, the young man progressed greatly through five months of training. It truly seemed as if he were an overcomer. He set aside his old patterns of drug abuse and poor self-esteem. However, after he left the mission and returned to work, he fell back into old habits and unwise friendships. The weak foundation of his early life came back into focus. He dwelled on his anger and bitterness, which led to serious trouble at his work, in his marriage—which ended in divorce—and even with the law. This affirms the importance of laying a firm foundation for our children while they are still young.

Unfortunately, many parents fail at this because of their own expectations and dreams for their children's lives. Bill and Sharon made that mistake with their son John. Bill was a successful pastor who devoted his life to the preaching of the Gospel. He and his wife, Sharon, raised two godly children. Bill was convinced that being a pastor was God's highest vocation for a man. In subtle ways, he communicated that message to John, who, out of respect for his father, enrolled in Bible college. Four years after graduation, John finally found the courage to be honest with his parents. He told them that he never had been motivated to be a pastor. At first his parents, especially Bill, were angry. Their expectations had been dashed. Their son would not be joining his father in the pulpit as they had assumed.

As Bill and Sharon prayed over their disappointment, they received revelation from the Lord. They began to see their mistake in assuming they knew what God had in mind for John. They repented to the Lord for detouring His purposes in John's life. They also apologized to John for imposing their dreams and expectations onto him, and released him to find God's purpose for his life.

Most of us have experienced similar situations within our families. Through our children's growing-up years, we often ride an emotional roller coaster. We flip-flop between wanting our children to grow up to be and to do what comes naturally to them, and wanting them to make us proud and to satisfy our egos. But our children are not trophies for people to admire or for puffing up our egos. Yes, wanting our children to do well is perfectly normal, but we must want it for their benefit, not ours. This latter perspective causes us to fall prey to using subtle manipulation to maneuver our children into fulfilling our expectations, not theirs.

Our children are not carbon copies of us; they are unique. God has invested in each child a blend of natural talents and abilities, motivational patterns and intellectual abilities that make that child different from anybody else who has ever been born. Our job as parents is to draw out the unique spark God has placed in each of our children. We must provide a nurturing environment in which they can grow and develop physically, intellectually, emotionally and spiritually. We must also help them recognize who they are and what direction best employs their unique arrangement of talents, gifts and motivations.

As parents, we are responsible for helping our children become all that God intends for them to be. And as Christian parents, we have no higher calling than accomplishing this goal. No greater sense of fulfillment can we experience than by its attainment. Though we may be fallible individuals, with God's help and wisdom, we can faithfully discharge the great responsibility God has granted us.

Getting to Know
Your Child's Design

The first duty of love is to listen.
Paul Tillich

CHAPTER TWO

*D*oes the job of figuring out your children and heading them in the right direction seem a little overwhelming to you? Relax, it's supposed to be!

God created us to be interdependent beings, assisting others as well as receiving help from them. Unfortunately, in today's society, interdependence has been overshadowed by independence. And in our independent, self-sufficient society, we often feel insecure about involving other people in our tasks.

The truth is, we need other people. And when it comes to figuring out the unique children God has blessed us with, we need a perspective larger than our own. If we do not seek that perspective, the task of raising our children becomes immeasurably more difficult, even jeopardizing our children's potential for making maximum use of all their wonderful skills and abilities.

Think of driving a car. The driver sits in the front seat of the car and looks forward through the windshield. That's how the driver is supposed to sit. But when facing forward, the driver can't see what is going on behind the car, and so must use a rear-view mirror. Since the driver needs to know what's going on behind the car, he or she is expected to frequently check the rear-view mirror, especially when turning or changing lanes. Regularly checking the rear-view mirror is one of the requisites of being a good driver. So it is in parenting our children.

Taking Advantage of Other People's Insights

No matter how good we as parents may be, we cannot see everything from where we sit. We need other people to act as rear-view mirrors for us. God surrounds us with a variety of people who can offer us a well-rounded perspective of our children and ways to best parent them. Needing such people is not an admission of failure or weakness, but is a sign that we recognize our own limitations.

Our children have the advantage of being observed in a variety of settings by a number of adults whose insights can help us understand and adapt our parenting style to our children. These adults can be youth leaders, Sunday school teachers, coaches, friends, neighbors, grandparents, uncle, aunts and the like.

Perhaps the most obvious adult with insight into our child's life is the child's school teacher. After all, teacher and child spend a substantial part of each day together. The teacher observes the child in a number of situations in which we are not involved. We should consult with the teacher from time to time about our child's progress at school, as well as about areas of improvement needed for our child's development. The teacher may notice certain gifts and qualities in our child that should be encouraged and nurtured. The teacher may be able to give us insights into how our child reacts in various circumstances and functions in different social settings. All of this presupposes that we are willing to listen to and accept what the teacher has to say. As our friend Rachel found out, that is not always the case.

Rachel was a first-year teacher at a public school in a rural community. Rachel's husband had recently been appointed as pastor of the local Methodist church, where about one-third of Rachel's second-grade class attended.

After training and working as a nurse for several years, Rachel had chosen to return to college to become a teacher. She had done well, graduating with honors and winning an award for her teaching abilities. She also had a genuine love for the children in her class, and wanted to see each child do his or her best. So Rachel spent a lot of time preparing for her first parent-teacher conferences, her opportunity to discuss her students' progress with their parents.

Rachel's first interview was with Jill's mother, who directed the church choir. Rachel wanted to discuss Jill's struggle with math, a struggle that could leave her lagging behind her classmates and facing the difficult task of catching up. As Rachel tried to share her concerns, Jill's mother admitted that she, too, had struggled with math. She filled the remaining conference time telling Rachel about her own failures at school and her theories as to why they happened. Rachel was dismayed. Jill's mother seemed more inter ested in talking about herself than in helping solve her child's problem.

Rachel's next interview was with Andrew's father. Andrew had been caught stealing at school—other children's pencils, stickers and other small items. Since Andrew's father was an elder in the church, Rachel was sure he would want to get to the bottom of the situation. But after tactfully explaining the issue, she was surprised when Andrew's father came up with excuse after excuse for his son's actions. It was as if he didn't believe his son was capable of stealing.

Rachel was only two conferences into the afternoon, and was already weary. The meetings were not turning out to be the cooperative, information-swapping, problem-solving sessions she'd imagined. And she hadn't yet spoken with Jason's mother!

Jason was particularly troublesome. Restless and unable to concentrate on his work, Jason attracted "followers" rather than friends. His bizarre actions gained their admiration, and Rachel feared the worst for him as he grew older. To make matters worse, when confronted in class about some unfinished work, Jason let forth with a string of expletives. Rachel felt compelled to have one last shot at honesty.

Rachel discussed Jason's deteriorating behavior, including the cursing incident, with his mother. Jason's mother looked calmly at Rachel and replied, "Oh, yes, Jason did tell me that you two have a personality conflict." Rachel couldn't believe what she was hearing. Disillusioned, she completed the rest of her parent-teacher conferences very superficially.

Later that afternoon, while Rachel sat emotionally drained in the staff lounge, the school principal strolled by and casually asked, "How did it go?"

Rachel shared her frustrations with the whole process. The principal smiled and said, "You learned something this afternoon. Parents want to hear only good things about their children. They come to these conferences for a pat on the back, for something to take home and brag about to their friends. If you don't give them that, they fight back."

Rachel wanted to say parents shouldn't react that way, but she didn't want to sound naive. Besides, two of the parents were Christians who were supposed to pray for their children and take an interest in their social and moral development.

Dejected as Rachel felt, ultimately the children were the real losers in these parent-teacher conferences. Rachel's insights coupled with the parents' experiences could have positively changed the children's lives.

It is difficult to hear negative things about our children. Nobody wants to hear that his or her child is not doing well in a subject, is being abusive or disrespectful or is socially isolated from his or her classmates. But if parents are not open to hearing and dealing with negative information, they and their children pay a price.

Several years after those first conferences, I asked Rachel, now a mother herself, how she approached parent-teacher interviews.

"You must realize," she said, "that your child's teacher is very unlikely to say anything specific or personal—that is, anything truly useful to you—unless you give them permission to do so. If you don't, it's simply not worth the risk for them."

Rachel asks her children's teachers the following:

(1) What are my child's easiest and most difficult academic areas?

(2) Do you feel that my child is working at his or her potential in all areas?

(3) What do you see as my child's greatest social and emotional strengths and weaknesses?

The most crucial step is to not ask questions, but to listen to answers, not always an easy task. We are tempted to rush in to defend or to excuse our child's behavior. If we control this urge, we'll find that most teachers will offer candid suggestions based on their observations. If you ask Rachel's three questions—and truly listen to the answers—you could gain tremendous insight into your child. You will have invited another adult who knows your child well to be your rear-view mirror.

Of course, like mirrors—which can sometimes distort what they reflect—teachers may not be absolutely correct about their observations. Thus, we advise bringing each insight before the Lord in prayer.

Beware of Tests

Another comment on teachers and schooling is to trust personal observations over test results. Since many things can skew test results, we should not put too much faith in tests alone. Our education system emphasizes grades, grade levels and IQ tests, but the average child will score at different levels in different subjects. A child may be good at spelling or reading, and poor at arithmetic or physical education.

A great weakness in American education, especially in public schools, is that children are placed into grade levels and expected to perform and conform according to standards set for each level. Such a system rarely recognizes how each child differs in learning to think and to read. Only twenty-five percent of fourth-grade students will actually be at grade level, and none will be at grade level in every subject.

My son Matthew started his education in a Southern California public school. In first grade, he was evaluated by a testing program that found him to be "markedly below average" in many of his subjects. My wife, Betty, and I knew that Matthew may have been a little behind in grasping some of the concepts he was to master in first grade, but from our observation of him at home, he was not below average. We set the test information aside until, in third grade, his test results deemed him "average." Test results in the following two years showed Matthew to be "above average," then "markedly above average." When Matt was in sixth grade, we were told he was gifted!

What Matthew needed was time to develop. Betty and I knew that the boy we observed at home—the boy we encouraged and nurtured—was not below average. That boy had many talents and abilities that needed to be drawn out and developed over time. After all, growing up is incremental, day-by-day physical, mental, emotional and spiritual growth and development. Of course, if Matthew's behavior at home had lined up with the test results, we would have pursued the various avenues open to help him overcome any learning difficulties. Time was all Matthew needed, and as it turned out, we knew our son well.

Sometimes, we parents must follow our gut instincts in raising our children. Diagnostic tests are not foolproof, but if we see by our child's behavior that help is needed, we must not let pride or embarrassment get in the way of seeking appropriate assistance. Our child's physical and mental well-being is more important than our pride.

Storing Insights Away

We are all familiar with the story of Mary and Joseph and the birth of Jesus. We remember how the angel announced Jesus' birth to the shepherds. In his gospel, Luke told us:

> *So they hurried off and found Mary and Joseph, and the baby, who was lying in the manger. When they had seen him, they spread the word concerning what had been told them about this child, and all who heard it were amazed at what the shepherds said to them. But Mary treasured up all these things and pondered them in her heart.* —Luke 2:16-19

We're not suggesting that our children are on the same level as Jesus, but there are times when God allows significant people to speak into our children's lives. Like Mary, we should take the time to treasure and ponder what is said. One of the best ways to do this is to keep a record for each child, using a simple notebook in which to write down events and people's insights and ideas about the child.

Rachel keeps a small cloth-bound book for each of her three children. She takes each child's book with her to parent-teacher conferences, and jots down notes while the teacher talks. Teachers who see their views taken seriously are more likely to tender other useful insights about our children.

Motivating Abilities

Looking back over the record of what God has shown us directly and what others have told us about our children allows us to see emerging patterns in our children. Things that bring joy and fulfillment or frustration and discouragement become obvious. As years pass, we notice that these things don't really change. The following passage from *Finding a Job You Can Love* describes these patterns this way:

> In our professional experience, evaluating thousands of individuals over twenty years, we have found that each person displays an entire behavior system, which we call a "motivational pattern," over and over again. In other words, we all have individual likes and dislikes. We react to people, things and circumstances in the same way time and again. We human beings are far more consistent in our thoughts, words and actions than we realize. Thus we say such things as, "Isn't that just like him?"

Since we all have motivational patterns, it's important for us as parents to help our children discover what God has placed within them. *Finding a Job You Can Love* has a useful appendix that describes the System for Identifying Motivating Abilities (SIMA) and presents an outline that explains these different abilities.

A simple test, SIMA requires observing a child's life and clearly identifying the things that bring the child the greatest amount of pleasure. The things the child likes to do are going to be those things that he or she is good at doing. As we help our child find pleasurable outlets, we begin to see how the child best functions. SIMA presents a long list of abilities that can be clearly identified: an investigative ability (to interview or experiment); a learning ability (to conceptualize, picture or dream); an evaluative ability (to analyze, assess and select); a writing ability (to edit, compose or advertise); and an ability to influence (to convince, advocate, motivate or sell).

Another helpful aspect of identifying motivational abilities is recognizing the types of objects our children work best with, such as figures, people, physical things, projects and words. Just as importantly recognized are the mechanisms through which they work, such as art, ideas, enterprises, systems or policies.

Finally, our children can discover whether they work best with others as team members; as team leaders, coordinators, directors, managers or coaches; or as individuals.

Discovering my children's motivational abilities has helped me to better understand them. It is important for one of my sons to gain recognition and attention. So as a parent, I have learned to readily give him the recognition he desires, instead of his having to go to extremes to be recognized by me.

I also have a daughter who likes to master and perfect things, a trait that appeared at a very young age. She would have been greatly frustrated had we made her hurry through tasks, telling her, "That's good enough." What was good enough for us would not have been good enough for her.

Discovering our child's motivational abilities pattern can greatly help us to understand our child, making us more effective parents. But we also need to discover each child's unique set of abilities that determine how the child processes information.

Intellectual/Learning Style and Capacity

Traditional thought tells us that intelligence is something a child is born with. A child's intellectual capacity can be mathematically calculated, quantified and represented as a number referred to as the Intelligence Quotient (IQ). A child's IQ is gauged using a series of questions that test the child's linguistic and logical-mathematical abilities. Recent theorists J.P. Guilford, Robert Sternberg and Howard Gardner have challenged traditional notions of intelligence.

In 1967, J.P. Guilford identified three facets of intelligence: mental operations (the process of thinking), contents (what we think about), and products (the end results of our thinking).

Howard Gardner of Harvard University suggests that in addition to linguistic and logical-mathematical abilities, there are five other forms of intelligence: spatial, musical, bodily-kinesthetic, and interpersonal and intrapersonal intelligence. Interpersonal intelligence is the ability to discern and respond appropriately to the moods, temperaments, motivations and desires of other people. Intrapersonal intelligence is a person's ability to access his or her own feelings, discriminate among them and draw upon them to guide behavior—a person's knowledge of his or her strengths and weaknesses.

Robert Sternberg's theory suggests that intelligent behavior is the product of applying thinking strategies, handling new problems creatively and quickly, and adapting to contexts by selecting and reshaping our environment.

Each of these men has not only challenged the old beliefs about intelligence, but has also provided a system of thinking to apply to the nature of intelligence. One such system is the Structure of Intellect (SOI), which was developed by J.P. Guilford and was applied to education by Mary Meeker through the Structure of Intellect-Learning Abilities (SOI-LA) test.

This test models how a child processes information in order to understand that intelligence is composed of many different types of thinking. The question to be answered is not *how much* but *what kind of* intelligence a child has.

The SOI-LA test evaluates three basic categories of thinking: mental operations, contents and products. The test assesses how a child's thinking is structured, then tries to ascertain the mental process of thinking used by the child. It also seeks to point out the kinds of content the child works with most naturally: figural (information in a concrete form), symbolic (information in a notational form such as letters and numbers that have an agreed-upon meaning) or semantic (dealing with concepts and ideas). The SOI-LA determines the end results of the child's thinking, or products.

While the SOI-LA assessment gives understanding on how a child's thinking is structured, the

SIMA, as previously discussed, discerns the motivating pattern that drives the child in the way he or she thinks. For example, a child who is not doing well at school might be assumed to be lazy or slow. In fact, the child could be an auditory learner in a classroom with a teacher who prefers to give written instructions and explains things diagrammatically rather than orally. Once we know this about a child, it is much easier to work with him or her to strengthen areas of weakness and to find other ways to effectively teach the child.

Nurturing Uniqueness

Because every child is designed by God to be a unique combination of genes that have never before existed and will never again exist, our job as parents is to nurture that uniqueness. We need to provide a safe place where our children can grow and develop into the people God made them to be.

Along the way, we need some understanding of our children's unique talents and abilities, some of which will be obvious to us, some of which will not. Some of our children's abilities may show up in settings away from the home, such as school, youth ac tivities and sports. We therefore need to solicit input from people who are involved with our children in these settings. In addition, various tests—two of which we have mentioned in this chapter—can evaluate a child's intellectual abilities and motivational patterns. Other tests measure personality types and give some clue as to each child's comfort able social settings.

As parents, we need to know each of our children. The information discussed in this chapter can help us weave the threads of information into a rich tapestry of knowledge and understanding that will continue to expand through the years as our children grow into adults. With the knowledge contained in that tapestry, we can lead, guide, encourage, teach and admonish each child to grow into the unique person God created him or her to be, and to find and to walk out the plan He has for each life.

Principles to Grow With

Principles are like the stars:
We never reach them,
but like the mariners of the sea,
we chart our course by them.
Carl Schurtz

CHAPTER THREE

*T*oday's children are growing up in a moral and spiritual vacuum. Stripped of any guiding principles, they wander through a wasteland of aimlessness, hopelessness and selfishness. The current crime epidemic, immorality, drugs and gang hatred are all symptoms of the disease that has blighted the soul of our nation and the souls of the young men and women growing up in it.

As Christian parents, our desire is to raise children who love God with their whole hearts and who want to affect the world around them with the gospel message. We must provide an environment for them to grow up in which ensures that they cannot be sucked into the moral and spiritual vacuum of the world. That safe environment is the family.

The family should be a loving, principle-centered place in which our children can grow safely and securely. Many Christian parents have intuitively provided such a home environment. As LeeAnn and I look back at the way we raised our children—she with Willard and I with Betty—we see that there were core principles that guided the way our families functioned. These principles were not always articulated well, but they were nonetheless in place.

LeeAnn and I have thought much about these principles. We have come to call them unifying principles, because that is what they do. They undergird the family, guide the actions of family members and hold the family together as a unit. They provide stability and security. They give our children a tool by which to measure situations and their reactions to them. More than ever, these principles need to be emphasized for our children because of the seeming lack of unifying principles guiding the social, moral, spiritual and political fabric of our nation.

One of the best ways to emphasize these principles is to articulate and put each in writing. Not only does this specifically lay out for our children the scope of the principle, but it helps us to clarify our thinking regarding it. Our children will also be enlightened if we lay out the reasons for and the consequences of not living by a particular principle.

Set out in the next few pages are a number of these unifying principles LeeAnn and I used while raising our families. You don't need to use them all, and you may have other principles you use that are not recorded here.

This list is not intended to be exhaustive, merely illustrative of the types of principles we are discussing and how they might apply to our families. One thing LeeAnn and I are sure of is that these principles have helped us raise children who love and serve

God and who want to touch the lives of other around them with the power of Christ's love.

Unifying Principles:
The Supreme Importance of Knowing God

Since knowing God through establishing a relationship with Him is the primary goal for every Christian, this principle should be first and foremost in every Christian home. Indeed, it is upon this principle that all other unifying principles are predicated.

Having and enjoying a personal relationship with God is what marks Christians as different from non-Christians. We Christians may do many of the same things as non-Christians in our homes and with our families. We can feel the same emotions, suffer the same illnesses, even attend the same church. But in their unsaved state, non-Christians cannot enjoy a relationship with God as we can.

We must teach our children from an early age— and teach them by example as well as by words—the supreme importance of knowing God through a personal relationship with Him. As our children grow, we need to guide them in how to develop their relationship with the Lord, just as we offer them guidance on how to make and relate to friends.

Personally knowing God forms the basis of stability and security within the family. The Christian family is founded upon this knowledge. It is the greatest spiritual inheritance we can leave our children.

Staying Humble

Nothing repels like arrogance and conceit, and nothing attracts like humility. Though Jesus was the exalted Son of God, He came to earth in obedience and humility, and wherever He went, people were attracted to Him. If we want our children to grow up to have strong Christlike characters, we need to ground them in humility. We need to teach and demonstrate that before all else, we must be clothed in humility.

God's Word has much to say about humility. In Matthew 18:4, God reminds us of the following truth: "Therefore, whoever humbles himself like this child is the greatest in the kingdom of heaven." In 1 Peter 5:5-6, He reminds us of His attitude to ward off humility with these words: "God opposes the proud but gives grace to the humble. Humble yourselves, therefore, under God's mighty hand, that he may lift you up in due time."

For me, humility is perhaps the greatest of all Christian virtues. It is the ground from which all other virtues and spiritual fruits grow.

Humility stands at odds with the self-sufficient, self-absorbed and self-centered spirit so prevalent today. Scripture points out that God opposes the proud but gives grace to the humble. Humility needs to guide our family relationships as well as those in the work place or at school. All our dealings with people need to be wrapped in humility.

Keeping It Simple

Simplicity is another value that stands at odds with the prevailing attitude of today's world. Simplicity was as important a value to the saints of old as it was to our nation's founding fathers.

Today, however, complexity greets us at every turn. Most often, complexity equates to busyness, whether at our job, at school or at home. We find ourselves constantly under pressure to meet deadlines and quotas, to keep appointments and to get our kids to their various extracurricular activities. If left unchecked, our home can begin to resemble a transit station.

Becoming so busy makes it easy for us to lose sight of our goals and purposes. It also becomes easy to lose sight of God's vision for our lives. Worst of all, we become so exhausted that we don't really care.

When we find ourselves in such a situation, it's time for us to slow down and do some serious evaluation. We need to get our eyes back on what is really important: our relationship with God and our relationship with our family. People are more important than frantic activity. What point is there in achieving all our goals and meeting all our deadlines if we lose our relationship with the Lord and with our children?

Simplicity needs to be a unifying principle in our families. If we want our children to grow up to serve God and change the world, we need to help them focus on the things that are truly central to maintaining their relationship with the Lord.

Being Good Stewards

We all acknowledge in our heads that all we have and are belongs to the Lord. When our children look at our lives and the way our family functions, do they see evidence of this? Or do they see us holding tightly to the things God gives us?

Luke told of one day in the temple when Jesus looked up and saw the rich putting their gifts into the temple treasury. He also saw a poor widow put in two very small copper coins. He made an interesting observation to His disciples:

> *I tell you the truth...this poor widow has*
> *put in more than all the others. All these*
> *people gave their gifts out of their wealth;*
> *but she out of her poverty put in all she had*
> *to live on.* —Luke 21:3-4

Any church treasurer or fund-raiser for charity will point out that those we classify as poor usually give the most. The rich may give larger dollar amounts, but the poor often outgive the rich by donating a larger percentage of their income. Somehow the more people have, the more they want and the more they tend to hold on to what they have.

Christians are not immune to this tendency. But how contradictory it is to the model Jesus left us! Wherever He went, Jesus shared openly with people, often meeting their physical needs.

While handling our finances in a God-honoring way and giving generously are important aspects of stewardship, being a good steward stretches well beyond our money. Peter told us, "Each one should use whatever gift he has received to serve others, faithfully administering God's grace in its various forms" (1 Peter 4:10).

Being a good steward means using all God blesses us with—money, talents and abilities—to serve and to minister to others. Each of us has been given specific abilities and talents. It's sad to see a mature Christian with little or no understanding of his or her specific gifts. How can this person assess how well he or she is doing to serve God if there is no clarity in what's to be done to serve others?

When Peter said, "Each one should," he was referring to Christians. In essence, all Christians should practice stewardship with all God has given them. Our home must become a place where stewardship is nurtured in our children until it becomes as natural to them as breathing. The best way to do this is by positive example.

When LeeAnn was a young mother, she took her sons shopping with her at Christmastime to buy and distribute gifts to the needy. Although each gift cost only a few dollars, it demonstrated to the boys that their parents, in their hearts and in their practice, were good stewards of what God had given them. Stewardship was a unifying principle in their family.

Being Faithful Servants

Servanthood flows straight from stewardship. Peter didn't tell us to give some of what God blesses us with to the poor and the needy; rather he told us to use those things to serve them.

Of course, serving others does not always come naturally. Most people would rather be served than to serve. This is especially true of children. But being served is not the way of God's kingdom.

In Acts 20:35, Paul reminded us of Jesus' words that it is more blessed to give than to receive. Our service to others is a tangible representation of God's love for them.

We need to instill the importance of servanthood into our children. If they learn to serve and embrace one another in love at home, the transition to serving others outside the home will be easy. Jesus came not to be served but to serve. How often those in authority tend to forget this principle of servanthood.

Keeping Short Accounts

Do not let the sun go down while you are still angry. —Ephesians 4:26

These are wise words from Paul. Many a relationship has ended because someone did not deal with anger felt toward another. The anger was buried inside until finally its poison seeped out, marring and destroying the relationship.

We live in a high-pressure world that teaches us it's okay to be angry and frustrated, to blow off steam in an attempt to reduce pressure and frustration. But it's not okay, and we had better not send such a message to our children.

Blowing off steam can only result in hurt and bitterness and even more frustration. Rather, we should teach our children to keep short accounts by resolving their differences with people when they arise. In so doing, they not only adhere to Paul's advice but also learn to live life free from the suffocating resentment and bitterness of stored anger. They can become beacons of light to those around them, showing what it is like to walk in the path of forgiveness, love and reconciliation.

Repentance and forgiveness are ways by which people resolve their frustrations and difficulties with others, thereby keeping short accounts. What better way can a child learn the value of actions than by parental example?

Parents who miss the mark and wrong their children must be willing to repent and ask forgiveness. More than anything we can say, such actions will motivate our children more quickly to do likewise.

Being Accountable

When LeeAnn and I got married, we committed ourselves to hold one another accountable to God and to how we measured up to His Word. Accountability liberated rather than restricted us.

Whether we like it or not, life is a cooperative venture. God did not create us as islands to be completely independent of each other. Yes, He gave us the ability to think, reason, make decisions and act independently. He also designed us to be dependent upon one another, that is, to be *interdependent.*

One of the ways we express interdependency is to make ourselves accountable to others. Not only does accountability provide safety and security for us, but it also stimulates and challenges us toward growth and maturity at all levels of life. By being accountable, we invite the input of other people as to how our life is measuring up. This input is especially vital to our spiritual growth and development.

Although we can recount the value of accountability, our children may not always see it as valuable, and may resist embracing it. Here we must again become living, breathing models of the principle we want to impart to them.

Each spouse must begin to be accountable to the other. When we receive information, we must respond with humility, even when what our spouse tells us is hard to receive. Since God may well be speaking to our heart through what our spouse says, we must listen carefully and reverently as we seek to discern His voice.

Children who see our example can learn this important principle and incorporate it into their lives.

They will grow up knowing how to balance independence with interdependence, thus demonstrating godly character.

Loving Thy Neighbor

*And now these three remain: faith, hope
and love. But the greatest of these is love.*
—1 Corinthians 13:13

The greatest force to move a man's heart, Paul at-
tested, is love. Love for God and for our fellow humans is the glue that holds the Church together. It is
also the glue that holds the family together. The family is an incubator in which children experience love
from their parents and learn how to love one another.

The evening news on television bears stark testimony to what happens when people don't know how
to love and respect each other. We watch with fear
and anxiety the wave of violent crime that is overtak-
ing our nation. We wish our leaders would enact
stricter laws and enforce harsher penalties. But these
are not the real solution to the problem. Teaching
people to love and respect each other is, and the best
place to do this is within the sanctum of the family.

Our children hold the future in their hands. We
have seen the sin and degradation inflicted upon our
society by a generation of people who have forgotten
how to love and respect one another. We owe it to our
children's future to teach them the necessity of loving
others. Love is, as Paul said, the greatest virtue.

Always Doing Your Best and Never Giving Up

Earlier in my life I tended to procrastinate. Even
when I got around to starting something, I usually
didn't finish it. I learned quickly, though, that if I

want to be successful in the world and for the kingdom of God, I had better follow through until I completed a task. I also learned that I need to do my very best work.

From early in life, our children need to learn the importance of always doing their best and not giving up until a task is completed. Today's generation too easily whiles away the hours by watching television, playing video games or listening to music. At the end of the day, young people have little to show for their time.

It is imperative that children learn the value of getting a task done in a timely and proper manner. Future employers will look for this quality, not for how high a person scored on the latest video game.

Perseverance and striving for excellence are principles which shaped and molded our nation, and continue to sustain it. If we want our children to positively affect the world, we parents must teach them the value of doing their best and never giving up.

Teaching the Importance of Prayer

We need to reinforce at every turn the supreme importance of prayer for our children. Through prayer, we demonstrate our dependence upon God and upon His guidance and provision for our lives.

While many Christian couples regularly pray together for their children and for their family's needs, they need to include their children in praying for both major and minor decisions. Our children learn through prayer that God is interested in all areas of their lives, and that wants us to bring all our needs to Him. Again, this can be best taught by their observing our personal prayer lives. Our actions will show our children how much we really believe in prayer.

Teaching the Importance of the Word

We need to teach our children to be dependent upon the Word of God for their responses to the many situations they will face in life. We need to encourage them to read the Bible daily. We also need to read the Bible together during family devotional times, such as at meals.

When decisions need to be made, all family members should be encouraged not only to pray, but to read the Word to learn God's leading for a situation. By doing so, children learn to apply not only prayer but also the daily searching of God's Word to obtain guidance for their lives.

Stressing the Importance of World Missions

If our aim is to raise children who want to follow God's destiny for their lives and who want to change the world by the power of the Gospel, we need to constantly stress the importance of world missions.

Missionaries need to become more tangible than the faded image of a face in an old photograph taped to our refrigerator door. We need to make them come alive for our children. We need to become actively involved in supporting missionaries financially, praying for them, writing to them, encouraging them and sending presents and care packages to them.

We can't expect our children to do great things for God if they don't see us actively supporting those who are already busy working for Him, both at home and overseas.

Recognizing Enemies to Family Unity

As we seek to apply unifying principles to our

families, we need to remember that in the world family, unity has its enemies. Humanism, one such enemy, basically tells our children that they should decide for themselves what is right or wrong, that they are the gods of their lives. Such an idea is the complete antithesis of Christianity, where God set in order principles and laws of living that are right because He made them.

We are not God, and we cannot determine what is right or wrong. Only God is wise enough, pure enough and just enough to make such decisions. Human choices all too often result in moral and ethical chaos with ensuing physical, emotional and spiritual pain and anguish. We must teach our children to recognize the humanistic spirit of our age, and to be awake to its subtle dangers. We must teach them to recognize, fight and defeat such wrong thinking.

Another enemy of our family is materialism. Making decisions based on greed rather than on necessity is an easy error. Everywhere we turn, some enticement appears, trying to motivate us to accumulate more. Often these enticements are aimed by the media at our children. We should be careful to protect them from the brainwashing of television, radio, newspaper and magazine advertising.

Over the years, LeeAnn and I made it a habit to ask people whether they made enough money. Only one of our friends responded that he made enough; everyone else needed "just a little more." Several of our family's unifying principles were aimed directly at diffusing this kind of thinking and replacing it with godly principles for handling money and material possessions. Those principles became the measuring stick by which we evaluated our financial decisions.

Developing Team Players

Children need to understand that they are part of a team. They play a key role in the family, and if they don't fulfill it, the whole family suffers. Meeting that role allows the whole family to function at its best, building self-respect and responsibility and bringing great personal satisfaction in the process. When Betty and I were raising our children, we used an acrostic to help us remember that everyone in a family is a team member: Together Everyone Accomplishes More—TEAM.

As a family grows together, it becomes obvious that it is made up of separate and unique individuals. By working together, people can create a family unit that recognizes and honors the unique personal strengths of each family member.

To teach our children the value of being team players, we must affirm the importance of being flexible and having realistic expectations. Children need to understand that life has hardships, and that endurance is a great developer of maturity.

In life, no one is immune to problems and heartaches. As team players, we can help each other endure hardships and overcome problems and heartaches. We can demonstrate God's mercy to one another and reflect His love toward others.

Establishing a Personal Relationship with God

Even more importantly, each family member must be encouraged to have a firsthand experience with God. God has no grandchildren. Each one of our children must establish his or her own relationship with the Lord. We can encourage our children, but we can't do it for them. As many heartbroken parents are well aware, if we force them into such a decision, Satan can very easily force them out of it.

The best way to encourage youngsters to establish their own relationship with the Lord is by modeling for them what it is like to have a daily, living relationship with the Lord of the universe. If we live consistently by the unifying principles we establish for our family, and if we pray continually for our children, they will want to call our God their God. They will want to establish their own relationship with Him. This was our testimony as LeeAnn and I raised our families, and it can be yours.

For many years, I made New Year's resolutions, but rarely did they affect my life. As a general rule, they only discouraged me because nothing much came out of them. Then a few years ago, our family began to build a set of principles that could easily be remembered and used as a guiding force in our lives. It greatly helped us when we made up an acrostic to use to remember the principles.

We also taught and continue to teach a lot on living principle-centered lives. Each Discipleship Training School that we teach at forms its own set of principles and its own acrostic. We have received excellent feedback on how helpful using acrostics is. Here are examples of phrases you might use to draw your family together as you unitedly serve God:

To *know God and make Him known.*
Obedience

Love
Openness and honesty
Virtue or truth
Enthusiasm

Humility
Intercessory prayer
Meditate on God's Word

Establishing a personal relationship with the Lord is only the beginning. As our children live and grow by our family's unifying principles, we will want to help them establish a vision for their futures and discern God's destiny for their lives.

A Sense of Value

*Values in parenting style
become crucially important
when children arrive on the scene.*

CHAPTER FOUR

*R*ecently, as I was waiting in a hotel lobby, a woman and her three-year-old son approached the lobby desk to check out. The rather frazzled-looking woman told her son to stand by their luggage while she went and paid for their stay. The woman took her place in line waiting to be served, and her son stood by the luggage for a moment before he began to tug on the largest suitcase. Gradually, he began inching the suitcase across the hotel lobby. "I think your mom wants you to stay over there," I said to the little boy.

"Oh no," he said, puffing out his little chest, "my mom wants me to bring this bag to her." The boy totally trusted that he was following his mother's instructions. So he went, grunting and groaning and heaving the huge suitcase ever forward.

Finally and proudly, he made it to the counter. But how surprised he was at his mother's reaction when she saw him. She turned around and grabbed the boy tightly by his arms. "I told you not to move," she shouted. "You stupid little kid. I don't know why I brought you in the first place. You've been nothing but a nuisance since we got here."

With that, she gathered up her things and dragged her son roughly out the door toward a waiting taxi. I caught one last look at the small boy's bewildered face. He had been prepared to go any length to please his mother, and now his desire to please her had only earned him her wrath. He was confused.

That mother may never know the full effect of her hasty judgment against her son. To that small boy, his mother was so important that all he wanted to do was please her. That is what he thought he was doing by dragging that huge suitcase across the hotel lobby to her. But his mother's response was anything but affirming. Instead of communicating love and appreciation to her son, her words and actions told him that she neither valued nor respected him.

A perhaps more shocking incident that illustrates this same point occurred recently in Chicago. Police on a drug raid discovered nineteen children living in appalling squalor. Their apartment windows were broken, and the children all slept on two dirty mattresses on the floor. They had to compete with the dog for food, and the apartment was littered with garbage and excrement. As police removed the children from the hovel, one child asked a female officer, "Will you be my mommy? I want to go home with you." This child's cry was for someone to value, love, care for and cherish her.

We have previously pointed out that God created us to be interdependent. Part of that interdependence is found in our common need to feel valuable, a feeling that was denied those nineteen Chicago children and the three-year-old boy in the hotel lobby. If we want to raise children who love and serve God wholeheartedly, we must take seriously our children's need to feel a sense of value in their lives.

Basically, there are three categories of value: intrinsic and extrinsic value, character-based value, and performance-based value. A good understanding of these three value types will help us grasp how to value our children and how to teach them to value each other.

Intrinsic and Extrinsic Value

The value of a physical object has two levels: the specific value of the stuff that makes up that thing (intrinsic value) and the value assigned to the thing from outside sources (extrinsic value). For example, the intrinsic value of the metals used in making a one-dollar coin would be about eight cents. But after these metals are minted into a specific design, the extrinsic value would be one dollar.

People also have these two levels of value. An estimated $40 to $50 could purchase the necessary chemicals and elements to make a human body. While that may account for the component costs of a person, that amount is not the extrinsic value of a human being. Indeed, the extrinsic value of humans is so high that it cannot be measured in monetary terms. Why? Humans have a high extrinsic value because they have been shaped in the likeness of God. The first chapter of Genesis declares that God made us, and that He breathed His life into us so that we could enjoy fellowship with Him. We are made in

God's image. We are valuable because we are likenesses of the greatest being in the universe.

We are also valuable because of the high price God placed on our salvation. Our salvation cost God the death of His very Son. God could have easily decided to rid Himself of mankind and start over again, but He didn't. When He looked at humanity, He saw something worth redeeming. He saw something of value that only His Son could save and redeem.

The extrinsic value of human beings is not a value they earn or deserve, but rather is a value bestowed upon them by God. Because of His endowment, human life is valuable. This is why people protest abortion, euthanasia and physician-assisted suicide. Such people believe that all life is created by God, and is therefore extrinsically valuable. As a result, they feel compelled to preserve human life, whether born or unborn, or even whether a person is unable to live according to a man-made standard, or does not want to continue to live.

Our children are valuable because God fashioned them in the womb and breathed His life into them, then entrusted these special lives to us. By virtue of being born, each of our children is valuable, and we are to affirm that value to them. Even if they were never to do anything, they still have value. And knowing they have value, children can feel a great sense of security.

Character-based Value

*Whoever tries to live right and be loyal
finds life, success and honor.*
—Proverbs 21:21 (New Century Version)

In a world where politicians consult public opinion polls before responding to a situation, we esteem and honor those men and women who, regardless of popular sentiments, remain true to their principles. We call them people of integrity, people of character. Strangely, in a world of sliding morality and relative truth, people of character are greatly valued.

As we raise our children, we should guide them in developing a strong and consistent character. We can best accomplish that by being a shining example of godly character to our children. For example, if a sales clerk undercharges us, we need to speak up and pay what we correctly owe. Maybe we receive too much change and need to return it, even if it's only a nickel or a dime. No amount is too small when character is involved. Also, when we see our children's character grow and develop, we should honor them for the steadfastness of their constitution.

The best way to nurture godly character in our children is to establish underlying principles (refer to the previous chapter) by which our family lives and upon which individual family members are encouraged to base their decisions. We recognize people of strong character by the choices they make. Given the situations they face, and according to the principles upon which they base their lives, such people make the best possible decisions and, once the decisions are made, stick to them.

As our children attend school and confront peer pressure, making the right choice will be very important, especially if they want to maintain a strong Christian witness. Our children will come to realize that as Christians, they are different, that they cannot always go along with what their peers embrace as acceptable. Because there is so much moral impurity in our society, what may seem natural and permissible to our children's friends may be sin in God's eyes. Homosexuality is a good example. It is presented by the media simply as an alternative lifestyle. But young Christians must know what God's Word says about sexual morality, and must understand the importance of not being involved in unnatural affection.

We must also teach our children that sometimes "the good is the enemy of the best." It's not that we tend to choose bad things, but that we sometimes settle for things that are good but not necessarily best. As we work with our children, we need to teach them the importance of making right choices in all that they say and do. By making correct decisions based upon the Word of God, they demonstrate a deep and solid Christian character.

We should also instruct our children about the importance of holiness—the ground in which Christian character is rooted. We cannot be whole Christians and whole people if we do not embrace holiness as God's standard for our lives. We learn about God's holy standard by reading His Word. What we learn from His Word, we should apply in our lives and impart to others, especially our children.

Performance-based Value

> *Whatever you do, work at it with all your heart, as working for the Lord, not for men, since you know that you will receive an inheritance from the Lord as a reward. It is the Lord Christ you are serving.* —Colossians 3:23-24

Just as the world values people of strong character and integrity, it also values people who are diligent. In a real sense, the ability to diligently perform all that one undertakes flows directly from one's strength of character. People with strong character will diligently apply themselves to whatever they do. Even if everyone else at work slacks off when the boss is not around, the diligent person does not go along with the crowd. The Christian knows that everything he or she does is done for the Lord. The Christian's diligence flows from his or her desire to please God.

Our children need to realize the importance of always doing their best and working hard. The key words, however, are "always doing their best." We must be careful not to confuse diligence and performance with perfection. We are each gifted with different talents, abilities and motivations. Some of us are well-coordinated and exhibit good motor skills. Some of us may suffer from degenerative or congenital diseases that inhibit our ability to perform. What is important is that we perform to the best of our abilities. Knowing that we have done our best with what we have is more important than comparing our performance with that of someone who may have more natural talent and aptitude. We measure ourselves by whether or not we do our best, never by what someone else does.

A diligent example is LeeAnn's oldest son, Mark, who loves basketball. At 5'7", Mark was considered too short by the game's standards to be a solid addition to any team. Despite his size, he worked hard to develop his skills. While attending a Spiritual Renewal Week service at a local church with his family, Mark was struck by the pastor's reference to a Bible verse that stated that without God's help, a person could not personally add one inch to his or her stature. The pastor advised members of the congregation to "do your best with what God gives you." Inspired, Mark persevered with basketball until, according to the biblical edict, his weakness became his strength. He went on to play with a team that toured New Zealand and Australia before joining his college basketball team. God honors diligence.

The Dangers of Comparing

Paul advises the Galatians on this very point: "Each one should test his own actions. Then he can take pride in himself, without comparing himself to somebody else, for each one should carry his own load" (Galatians 6:4-5).

One of the most damaging things we can do to a growing child is to constantly compare the child with other children, especially with siblings. Confidence comes from who a child is, not how he or she compares to someone else. Some children are introverts, while others are extroverts. Not all children are athletic. Not all children can perform well on reading or math tests. Not all children are musical or artistic. We need to help our children see that they each have their own talents, gifts and abilities. Just as each person's fingerprints are unique, each person's whole being is unique.

Differences in Learning Styles

Not only are children different in their abilities, but they learn in different ways. Some children learn best by doing things with their hands, others learn best by seeing a skill demonstrated for them, and still others learn best by listening to something being explained to them. Normally, children use all three of these ways to learn, but they will tend to favor one approach as their primary form of learning.

For example, let's look at how we learn to spell. How do we best remember a word's spelling? Do we have to write the word ourselves? Do we have to see someone else write it? Or do we best learn the word when we hear someone spell it aloud? One of these ways will probably help us more than the others in learning to spell a word.

The same is true for children. When learning to read, for instance, each child will learn in his or her own way. Some children remember almost everything they read because they have photographic memories. Others may have very few phonetic skills, and so have difficulty sounding out words. In the end, they all learn to read; they simply follow different learning paths to acquire the skill.

All this points out that every child is special in his or her own way. Because each child is endowed with different insights, understandings, reactions and giftings, each needs to be treated differently from others. As parents, we must nurture this uniqueness in our children, adapting the way we work with them to maximize their potential. Every child deserves to be encouraged by his or her parents for this uniqueness, and not to be compared to and criticized for not being more like others.

Through focusing on our children's uniqueness and encouraging them to do their best, we can instill in them a sense of value.

Valuing Our Children and Teaching Them to Value Others

Understanding that our children are valuable is essential to their growth. Understanding the ways our children are valuable can help us nurture them. Perhaps if the mother of that small boy dragging the suitcase across the hotel lobby had encouraged his effort to please her, she could have reinforced just how much she valued him. But her inability to show her son that she valued him left him feeling confused, alone and unappreciated.

We must value our children if we want them to grow up to love and serve God. We must teach them that life is valuable, and that people are very important to God.

Our children need to know that God requires them to take their eyes off themselves and look at other people. If they do not come to value other people as God values them, they will see little point in reaching out and ministering to others. Other people will just not seem that important.

Our children need to know that people are valuable—so valuable, in fact, that God sent no less than His own Son to secure their salvation; so valuable that He commands us, as His children, to reach out and minister to people's physical, emotional and spiritual needs. People are on top of God's agenda because they are valuable to Him.

As we value our children, we offer them a key to developing a sense of vision for their lives. If children understand the importance of valuing others, they can be motivated to search for God's destiny for their lives, inspiring them with vision for how God can work through them to touch the lives of others (discussed further in chapter 5).

Honoring Our Children

Have you ever overheard someone praising you for who you are or for something you did? When you heard what was said, most likely you felt valued because you were being honored before another person. Being honored is supposed to make us feel valued, two concepts that are very closely aligned. We honor what we value. Honor has to do with recognizing value. Honoring is the way we communicate that someone or something is valuable.

We should be showing our children that we honor them. We should be encouraging them each day. It is said that people often become what we say they will become. What do we want our children to become? If we want them to grow to love and serve God, we need to tell them they are valuable to us and to the Lord.

Deuteronomy 5:16 tells us to honor our father and our mother. Great damage is done in families that do not honor their parents. We are responsible for teaching our children to honor their parents, and parents in return need to honor their children.

Our children learn by watching us. Are we teaching them to honor us by honoring our own parents, their grandparents? Do we look after our parents' needs? Do we honor our parents by visiting them regularly? Do we honor them with our words and our deeds? Are our homes full of photographs of our parents? Ask yourself this question: Are your children learning to honor you through your example of honoring your parents? Do your children know that you love and respect your parents?

Our children are God's gift to us. They are precious to Him, and they should be precious to us. We need to let them know they are valuable to us as well as to God.

One of the most effective ways to honor our children is through affirming and encouraging them. It is easy as parents to show our frustration with our children, and to openly criticize and even ridicule them. Such behavior only leaves them feeling devastated. When we find it necessary to correct our children, we should do so gently and sensitively, making sure we balance any negative observations with praise. We should also make sure any correction is done in private, never in front of friends or in public. When we are in public with our children, we should use affirming and encouraging words. Doing so not only affirms our child's value as a person, but also motivates our child to live up to the respect and honor being shown to him or her.

This doesn't mean we should never discipline our children. Every child needs to be disciplined at some point in his or her life. It is important, however, to understand why we discipline our children: We discipline them because we consider them to be so valuable that our failure to discipline them would be tantamount to not honoring them.

Discipline is a way of showing our children we love them. We do our children no favors when we fail to discipline them when the need arises, or when we choose to overlook obvious behavior that needs to be addressed and corrected. We must never forget that the purpose of discipline is to bring correction to our children's lives, not to visit vengeance upon them. Therefore, discipline must be fair, appropriate to the infraction and sensitive to the child's needs and feelings. Discipline must be administered with the point of enlightenment in mind. If it is not, our actions can often seem harsh and unreasonable to the child, causing the child to feel frightened, confused and not particularly valued.

Another way we can honor our children is by simply being there for them when they are emotionally hurt, when they face difficulties or when they just want to talk. Being available to listen to them and responding sensitively to their needs says much to our children about their value to us, particularly as they are growing up. We can honor our children by listening to their ideas and opinions without judging, although we need also to honor them by gently pointing out to them when an idea or opinion conflicts with God's Word.

Yet another way to honor our children is by keeping our promises and commitments to them. If we promise to be at one of our child's ball games or to attend a school production to see our child perform, we had better follow through. I am sure you know how it feels when someone fails to keep his or her promise to you. When this happens, most likely you feel unimportant and of little value to the person who made the promise.

When you make a promise to any of your children, be prepared to keep it. This is especially true for fathers. Men are so easily caught up in their careers that they allow their work to take precedence over their children. When that happens, fathers are conveying to their children that a job is more important than the child is. Fathers may not consciously think that, but their actions speak as much. Indeed, many fathers inadvertently alienate and devalue their children by placing too much attention and energy on their job and not enough on their children. And it's not wise to use the excuse, "My work is what pays the bills and puts food on the table." Most children are more impressed with the time their fathers spend with them than with their fathers' paychecks.

"Do to others what you would have them do to you," Jesus told us in Matthew 7:12. This truth should rule all our actions, especially in valuing our children. The need to be valued is universally felt. What do we want people to do to us and for us that affirms our value? That is what we ought to be doing to and for our children to affirm their value. And what makes us feel unimportant and devalued? That is exactly what we ought not to be doing for and to our children. It is that simple.

If they love the Lord, our children are co-heirs with Him. And if they are gifts from God and are co-heirs with Christ, they are valuable to Him as well as to us. Our job as parents is to help our children recognize their value through affirmation. Nothing will move a child forward into seeking God's vision for his or her life more than recognizing that he or she is valuable to God and that God wants the child to value other human beings just as the child's parents value the child.

A Sense of Vision

*Enthusiasm finds the
opportunities, and energy
makes the most of them.*

Chapter Five

At twenty-eight years of age, Chad was six years into his career as a financial consultant. One day as we ate lunch together in a local restaurant, Chad told me why he had chosen that particular career position. His interest started when he showed promise in math in grade school. His parents, who had lived through the Great Depression, thought his math ability could lead to some type of stable career in finance. They knew that such a career would enable him to provide for his family much more easily than they ever had been able to provide for theirs. As time went by, it was assumed that Chad would move into a career in finance. Chad made good grades in high school and went on to college, where he met Susanne. After college, the young couple married and had three children.

"You know, Duane," Chad confided in me, "I feel totally trapped, like I'm not really living. A part of me wants to throw it all away and do something adven turous. I'd like to travel, learn about different cultures and...oh, I don't know...maybe do some work with refugees or something. I'd like to be affecting people more directly with the Gospel. I know I help people in my job, but it's just not where I want to be."

"You must have thought about this before now," I said. "What's stopping you?"

Chad grimaced. "Everything. We're heavily mort-gaged, and the whole family is so used to my pay-check that they can't imagine my changing jobs. And I guess it wouldn't be fair. When Susanne and I mar-ried, I was on my way up the corporate ladder. How can I switch on her now?"

I wasn't sure what to say, so I nodded, and Chad went on.

"I guess I have to stick with things the way they are. I just wish I'd done something that felt like more than just a job—more than just a way to bring in a paycheck every week."

As we finished our lunch, we looked at some of the options open to Chad. Almost all of them re-quired some major life adjustments, not just for him but for his whole family. Chad left the restaurant with some hard choices ahead of him.

Chad is typical of many Christian young people I've met over the years. They seem to be doing the "right things," but they don't have any sense of expec-tation, any sense that they're living in God's will.

Like Chad, so many of these young people have been steered into career choices by their parents. Often these choices say more about the parents' de sires for their child than about the child's desires. And once locked into a career choice, many young people feel trapped. They find themselves toiling in a job that doesn't fulfill them and doesn't draw out of them all that God designed them to be. Chad may have had an aptitude for numbers, but he had a heart for serving the needs of people in ways other than by giving them financial advice.

It is not unreasonable for parents to have hopes and desires for their children. It *is* unreasonable, however, for parents to push their children into making long-term choices about their lives that fulfill only the parents' hopes and desires.

You'll recall the earlier discussion about how each child has his or her individual design, and how our job as parents is to discover and nurture that design. Part of the process involves gradually allowing our children to make more and more choices for themselves, including those choices about their careers. Certainly, by our example and by helping them to better understand themselves, we can give our children guidance. But we cannot force them to do what we wish they would do.

The simple fact is that a person will enjoy true fulfillment in a career choice only when he or she finds work that fully involves the person's unique set of talents, abilities and motivations given by God. That was Chad's frustration. Chad wasn't fulfilled as a financial consultant. His job may have tapped into his aptitude for numbers, but it didn't involve or satisfy any of his other talents, abilities and motivations. Chad knew that there was more, that by applying his skills to different situations, he could find much greater satisfaction and fulfillment. He could also see that his involvement in those activities could touch and change other lives as well.

Chad was beginning to grasp a sense of vision for his life. Unfortunately for Chad, he had already made major decisions that he felt locked him into work that he was less than enthusiastic about doing, and that locked him out of fulfilling his vision for his life.

Vision is defined as "sense of sight; supernatural apprehension; foresight." Not only do these terms define the word, but they describe the process whereby we apprehend God's vision for our lives. First, we see who we are—what talents, abilities, motivations, personality and physical attributes God has given us. Second, we ask God what He wants us to turn our attention to. Given the type of person He has made us, we ask Him what He wants us to accomplish. And third, understanding what God wants us to do with who we are, we make choices that will bring it to pass. Vision is knowing what we were made for and how we are going to achieve it.

In 1963, a young man stood before a crowd in Washington, D.C., and summarized the vision that guided his life: "I have a dream.... " Dr. Martin Luther King went on to give an articulate and stirring speech, one that has been often repeated to the present generation, and is likely to be repeated to many future generations.

Early in his life, Dr. King came face to face with racism in America. As time went by and young King discovered more about himself—his strengths and weaknesses, his talents and abilities—he began to see that just as God had called his father to become a pastor, God was also calling him. But beyond just being a pastor, King saw that God wanted him to use his talents and abilities to stand up for justice and equality. And Dr. King stayed faithful to the vision God had given him. He dedicated himself to the task. Eventually, he was brutally murdered as he sought to bring his vision to fulfillment.

Martin Luther King had a vision, a dream, and it guided his life at every turn. God has a vision for our lives and for our children's lives. Our job as Christian parents is to help our children discern what that vision might be.

The world is in desperate need of people with God's vision, people who will minister God's love, care and concern to it. The world is ripe for change. Everywhere we look, on every continent and in every nation, the world is falling apart. Societies are bursting at the seams with violence, corruption, poverty, disease, disasters, crime and every imaginable manner of evil. It is time for godly men and women to stand up and say to the world, "I have a dream..." and then set about changing the world through the power of the Gospel.

God wants all of us to be directly involved in this, and He most assuredly wants our children to grow up to be world-changers. He wants them to grow up with the fire of His vision and destiny for their lives burning within. And He wants us, as parents, to be involved in bringing this to pass in our children's lives. The obvious question is, How can we help our children find and develop that vision for their lives?

First, we need to follow through on what was discussed earlier in the book. We need to take time to discover what our children are really like: Not what we wish they were like, not what we hope they'll be like, but what they're really like. We must seek to understand the gift God has given us. What are our children's motivations? What are their talents and abilities? How do they best learn? What kind of social setting do they thrive in? Are they individualists or collaborative team players? We should know all of these things about our children. God has invested with us a treasure in the form of our children, and we need to discover the treasure He has given us. When we understand the make-up of these unique individuals, we are in a better position to know how to help, encourage and challenge our children to become all that God has created them to be.

Second, we should surround our children with godly principles designed to draw the family closer to the Lord and to develop Christian character. We should also help our children see and value things from God's perspective. If we remain consistent in these things, we will move our children a long way toward apprehending God's vision for their lives.

But there is still more we can do. Children love to dream about the future. They like to pretend that they're a firefighter, a doctor, a police officer, a nurse, an astronaut, a mom, and so forth. We adults love to watch the minds and imaginations of our children at work. We even encourage them by buying them related toys and books. We might buy a fireman's hat for our son or a medical kit for our daughter.

Not very long ago, one of our daughters-in-law decided that the best way to help her young son better understand how the fire department works was to take him to the fire station and let him experience it firsthand. To do this, she had to interrupt her busy schedule, but the great joy that her son received by actually visiting with firemen and seeing a fire station up close was well worth her effort. We might read our children stories or let them watch videos or television programs that not only inform their young minds, but also encourage them to use their imaginations to dream of what they could do in life.

Dreams and visions are all a natural part of a child's growing process, one that we need to carry over into the arena of faith. We need to fire our children's imaginations to dream about what they can do for God: Perhaps they can be a teacher, a doctor, a relief worker in an overseas country, or a pastor, youth director or evangelist. The options are endless. We can read stories to our young children of great men and women of faith. We can tell them stories about Abraham, Moses, Joshua, Ruth, Hannah, David, the apostles Peter and Paul, William Carey, C.T. Studd, Hudson Taylor, Mother Teresa, Charles Spurgeon, David Brainard, William Booth, Florence Nightingale, Brother Andrew, Bruce Olson, Loren Cunningham, Harriet Tubman, and the list goes on. Some stories about these people are found in the Bible, others in autobiographies and biographies, and still others in videos and movies.

The reason so many young people end up like Chad, trapped in an unfulfilling vocation, is that they have never been told it's okay to dream outside of society's accepted norms for adults. They've never been told that they can dream of working with the poor or ministering to the spiritual needs of people or tending to the medical maladies of tribesmen in some far-off place. And if we don't tell them it's okay to think that way, they probably won't. They most likely will follow the well-worn paths society has marked out into "traditional" vocations.

Of course, many of us may have issues to deal with in our own lives before we're comfortable about encouraging our children to think freely. Parents, whether Christian or non-Christian, are products of society and its traditions. Often we find it difficult to think outside these traditions, which translates into great difficulty in releasing our children to pursue certain vocations they perceive as God-given. Indeed, some parents have actively sought to dissuade their children from pursuing non-traditional vocations. This topic is explored further in the next chapter, but for our present purpose, let me just note that parents may need to do some heart searching before they are ready to encourage their children to dream about what they can be and can do for the Lord.

God's Vision for Our Children

In Proverbs 29:18 (New Century Version), Solomon pointed out: "Where there is no word from God, people are uncontrolled, but those who obey what they have been taught are happy. "

I like the way this version translates that verse. There are many young people, and not so young people, in the Church today who are uncontrolled. They may call themselves Christians, but they are not fully submitted to Christ's control. Being under His control, according to this verse, is premised upon hearing His Word to us.

One of the most important things God wants to communicate to our children is His vision of what He has created for them to do with their lives. His vision is not a vision of what someone else thinks would be right for our children; it is a vision tailored by God to perfectly suit our children's personalities and talents.

Our job is to help our children discover God's vision for them so they will not be uncontrolled. Instead, they will be focused on what God wants them to do with their lives. As the verse points out, those who obey what God has committed to them will be happy.

Helping a child discover and develop a vision for his or her life doesn't mean that by age twelve we have mapped out a plan for the child's entire life. Just because a young boy puts on a toy fire helmet and pretends he's a fireman doesn't mean we are to immediately lock the child into that vocation and start making choices that will start him on his way to becoming a fireman. Instead, we watch him grow and develop and learn more about himself.

The little boy who used to pretend he was a fireman and announce his career choice to everyone who came to the house may now show the desire and aptitude to be a civil engineer. We can take him to visit building sites around our city to let him observe engineers at work. We can encourage him to talk to engineers and ask them questions. Perhaps through these experiences our son will discover that he really doesn't want to be an engineer. He may begin to think about some other vocational choice. Or perhaps he will discover that being a civil engineer is exactly what he wants to do.

As his parents, we can guide his choice to mesh with his talents, abilities and motivations. We help our son pursue the matter further by searching out colleges that offer the best degree program for civil engineers. We find out the entrance requirements and costs to attend, and we work with our son toward meeting those requirements and costs. We help him choose the appropriate high school classes. We take him to the library or buy him books about engineering so he can begin to learn more about the principles and fundamentals of engineering. Then finally, one day, our son graduates and goes to work as a civil engineer. Getting him there was a very natural process. We helped, supported and encouraged our son, but we didn't push him into a career he didn't really want.

Our children can use this same process to become aware of a sense of vision for their lives. Such awareness comes about as part of the natural process of physical, mental, emotional and spiritual growth. We must continually encourage the process.

One of the best ways to encourage vision development in our children is to expose them to a wide range of ministry and mission opportunities.

A doctor friend who has been on outreach to Haiti a number of times decided to take his twelve-year-old son with him on his most recent trip. He pointed out that the trip said more to his son about using his talents and abilities for the Lord than anything he could have told him. Not only did his son learn about using his gifts for the Lord, but he also saw firsthand some of the world's tremendous human needs, needs that God has instructed us to minister to in His name. That trip provided important missions exposure to my friend's son and gave him something to think about and further analyze. And it planted seeds in the boy's heart that over time the Holy Spirit can nurture.

When my son Mark was about ten years old, I took him to visit an orphanage in Mexico. That trip had such a profound effect on Mark that twenty years later, he returned to the orphanage with an outreach team of young people to minister.

We can all do such things that expose our children to the many and various ways of sharing Christ's love. Families can get involved in one of many short-term mission opportunities. What better way to spend spring break or a week of summer vacation than by ministering to the poor in Mexico or Haiti or another needy country in Central America or the Caribbean? What about becoming involved with a ministry that cares for the poor and needy right in our own cities? The possibilities are endless for providing children with exposure to missions and ministry.

Becoming involved as a family in such activities is important because our children see that we place such a great value on these activities that we are prepared to become involved in them ourselves. As with most things to do with raising our children, leading by example is so much more effective in communicating the importance of something to them than simply telling them that it is important. For many years, LeeAnn and her first husband, Willard, were very involved in a singing ministry. Often on Sunday morning, the whole family got up very early and traveled long distances to sing. This spoke volumes to the children of their parents' love for God and the importance of engaging in ministry.

If we don't show our children by our actions that we truly believe having a vision for our lives is important, how can we expect them to have their own visions? Scripture points out that we reap what we sow. Unless we sow the seeds of vision in our children's hearts by our example, we will not reap the harvest we desire. We cannot lead a person further than we are prepared to go. God wants to use our children, but He wants us to lead them to Him. Not only does He want to use our children, He also wants to use us. We, too, must become actively involved in pursuing our own vision for our lives.

Another way to fuel vision in our children is to provide them with opportunities through which they can experiment with their gifts and talents. Perhaps, for example, one of our children feels that God might be calling him or her to become a pastor. Before running out and enrolling the child in seminary, we can arrange for the child to get some hands-on involvement with a pastor. Perhaps for a week during summer vacation, the child can accompany our own pastor or another pastor in our area to observe, experiment and discover for himself or herself whether pastoring best employs that child's talents and abilities. If the child discovers that this is what God is calling him or her to do and it meshes with who God has made the child to be, he or she can move ahead with confidence, making choices and plans necessary to fulfill his or her vision.

My friend Jeff wishes that such exposure had been offered to him. Jeff felt that being a pastor was God's vision for his life, and he spent five years training for the position, only to give up several weeks be fore his ordination. "I hated it," he said. "My personality and my motivations just weren't suited to being a pastor. It was a real struggle for me, and with the ordination looming on the horizon, I couldn't stand the pressure anymore. I didn't want to be locked into the role of a pastor for the rest of my life." Finally Jeff confided, "I wish I had thought about all the implications more before I ever started my training. I guess if I had, I probably wouldn't have started."

Finding that he wasn't suited to being a pastor wasn't the end of Jeff's ministry. Jeff simply hadn't properly focused on God's vision for his life, and soon after abandoning his pastoral career, he became a missionary, serving successfully in a number of capacities in several countries.

Hands-on experience can help our children avoid the pitfall that Jeff found himself in. Perhaps spending time with a pastor will help our son or daughter discover that his or her talents would be better employed as an evangelist, relief worker or missionary. The child can then make the necessary adjustments to pursue that vision. And in doing so, the child may find that he or she is still better suited to some other task that can be undertaken.

God uses this process in the lives of our children. Our part is to lead, support and encourage our children and provide them with opportunities to discover their destiny in life. Our job is to provide our children with a vision-enhancing environment in which to grow.

Helping our children develop vision for their lives is not an exercise in promoting their dreams or needs. Rather, it involves helping them to integrate their personal abilities and limitations within God's plan to accomplish what needs to be done. The vision we want our children to take hold of is a vision for their future that is centered not only around their personal ambitions but also centered around God's calling and gifting in their lives, if only to bring glory to Him.

People of vision are the ones who end up changing the world. Martin Luther King had a vision for the African-American population in the United States. In pursuing his vision, he changed the fabric of American society. He brought racial bigotry and hatred to the forefront to be addressed and dealt with. The apostle Paul had a vision—to take the Gospel to the "regions beyond" (2 Corinthians 10:16). Paul's desire—to see the Gospel preached in all the places it had not yet been preached—changed the world. The fact that we are Christians today attests to the potency of Paul's vision, one that carried him through many trials and hardships.

God wants men and women today who have a potent vision of what He wants to do with and through their lives. He seeks people who will stay committed to their vision, people who are willing to endure trials and hardships along the way to seeing their vision become a reality. He is looking among our children for these visionary people. He is looking for a new generation of young people to come forth who are committed to His ways, and He wants to use them to change the world. Our children can become world-changers. They own the future and, with burning vision in their hearts, can make that future glorious and godly. Our broken-down world doesn't have to stay broken-down. God wants to use our children to fix it, to minister to it, to cleanse it, to heal it and to breathe the new life of the Spirit into it.

As parents, are we ready to cooperate with God in this venture? Are we willing to encourage and guide our children as they discover God's vision for their lives? Are we going to let our children become trapped by the ordinary, as Chad was trapped, or are we going to release them to become world-changers for God? I pray that our answer is "yes," and that every day we spend raising our children burns into our hearts the words of Proverbs 29:18. The world is ready for a new generation of men and women of God.

Praying for Our Children

The most powerful activity you can participate in is prayer. That is why you need to think through what you are praying for another individual. Nothing so moves the circumstances of life as prayer does.

Charles Stanley

CHAPTER SIX

*I*n our modern society, with its focus on instant gratification and instant solutions to problems, prayer is usually the loser. Even within Christian circles, prayer is often viewed as the domain of saints and the hyperspiritual.

Prayer is the first thing to go from our hectic schedules, when the opposite should be the case. The busier we become, the more we need to pray, seeking God for wisdom on the various situations we face, drawing our strength from and resting in Him. Too often, we forge ahead in our own wisdom and strength, often harried, frustrated, and never feeling we are getting anywhere. Prayer—not more grit, determination and human effort—is our answer.

With our family, prayer, too, is the answer. Raising children to love and serve God with a whole heart is not easy in today's world. We can study all the principles, techniques and programs put forward for accomplishing this task, but unless we bathe the whole endeavor in constant prayer, we are destined for failure. The process can be accomplished only with the Holy Spirit's agency and help. We should constantly turn to Him in prayer, asking for His wisdom and His insight into our children and how we should respond to and encourage them. And we should ask and release Him to work in our children's lives.

God has a special place in His heart for children. We adults are admonished to become like little children. Jesus spent time with children to show them His tender love. In Mark 10:14, Jesus said, "Let the little children come to me, and do not hinder them, for the kingdom of God belongs to such as these." Mark went on to tell us that Jesus took the children in His arms and blessed them.

The future belongs to our children, as does God's kingdom. Since we raise our children to seize and shape the future, we need to raise godly men and women who are rooted firmly in a personal relationship with Jesus Christ, and whose character is exemplary. We need to raise our children to become adults who are convinced of the life-changing power of the Gospel. We need to raise them to take the Gospel and apply its life-changing message to every area of society, fashioning a just and righteous future for the world and extending the borders of God's kingdom in the process.

To raise such children is more than we can do in our own strength. We need the agency of the Holy Spirit at work in our lives and in our children's lives. The best way to release Him to work in all of us is through prayer: We need to pray often and fervently for our children.

How do we pray effectively for our children? The following sections discuss several elements of effective prayer.

Pray in Faith

For our prayers to be effective, we must have the kind of faith Jesus talked about in Mark 11:23: "I tell you the truth, if anyone says to this mountain, 'Go, throw yourself into the sea,' and does not doubt in his heart but believes that what he says will happen, it will be done for him."

We must be convinced that God is in control. Unless we believe that God has a purpose and a design for our lives and for our children's lives, our prayers will go no further than the ceiling. The first and foremost ingredient in prayer is faith.

There was a time when two of our three children were not walking closely with the Lord. It grieved my wife, Betty, and me greatly. We were so tempted to nag and try to coerce them into coming to church with us, but Betty decided the best way to tackle the problem was through prayer. Betty loved to meditate on the Word, and soon after her decision to intercede for our children, she read, "All your sons will be taught by the Lord, and great will be your children's peace" (Isaiah 54:13). Betty took this to be a promise to her from the Lord.

We began to pray and to recite that Scripture. Before long we noticed a change beginning in each of the children. Within a short time, each one reached the point of deciding to make things right with the Lord. From that time on, they never looked back in their relationship with God.

We should pray faithfully for our children, believing that God can reach and touch their lives and draw them to Him.

Pray with Patience

> *Then the Lord replied: "Write down the revelation and make it plain on tablets so that a herald may run with it. For the revelation awaits an appointed time; it speaks of the end and will not prove false. Though it linger, wait for it; it will certainly come and will not delay."* —Habakkuk 2:2-3

We humans haven't changed much since Habakkuk's day. We want answers right now! When God gives us a promise for our children, we want to see it come to pass immediately. That's not always what happens, however. The Lord reminded Habakkuk that even though the promise may seem slow in coming to pass, at the right time it will happen, and it will happen quickly.

God's vision is not constrained by time, as is ours. Since it may take years for the promise the Lord has given us for our children to be worked out in their lives, we shouldn't get too frustrated over the different ways in which they develop. As LeeAnn and I look at the children we raised, we see that they all developed at their own pace, yet God brought His promises to pass in their lives at the right time.

As parents, we must become patient prayers, learning to be content to present our requests to the Lord and to wait on His answers. Many times, though, we are not patient. When something does not come to pass in the time frame we think it should, we stop praying. But we stop too soon. Just because God doesn't answer our prayers immediately doesn't mean He doesn't hear them.

God's ways are infinitely higher than ours, and we don't want to limit Him to our small view of the way we think things should be. We want His promise brought to fruition at the proper time, and we must become content to wait for that appointed time. If we get ahead of the Lord, we may put undue pressure on our children, perhaps causing them emotional and spiritual damage.

Pray as the Watchman of Your Children's Souls

> *Parents generally pay vigilant attention to the type of friends with whom their children associate but do not exercise a similar vigilance regarding the ideas which the radio, the television, records, papers and comics carry into the protected and safe intimacy of their homes.* —Pope John Paul II

> *How can anyone enter a strong man's house and carry off his possessions unless he first ties up the strong man? Then he can rob his house.* —Matthew 12:29

God has given us parents the responsibility and authority to pray for our children. In our evil and degraded society, we need to constantly pray a hedge of protection around our children. We are the protectors of our families, and figuratively speaking, we need to stand in the doorways of our homes and say to all forms of evil that try to enter, "Stop! In Jesus' name you will not come into my house."

One of the best ways I know to pray with this kind of authority is to pray from the Word of God. When we pray from the Word, we know we're praying in accordance with God's will. Thus, we should read and study His Word and allow Him to speak to us through it. When we pray the Word that God gives us, we pray with faith and authority.

One particular area we should aggressively pray over is the media, a powerful influence in our children's lives today. Prior to the media explosion over the past several decades, information rested with older people, who passed it on to the young and, in doing so, influenced the present. Today there is no drawing on the past, only emphasis on now and the future.

The world is changing rapidly because of the media. Tragically, most media forms are under the control of non-Christians. Thus, as Pope John Paul II reminded us, we must diligently guard our children from the media's ungodly influences. As Christians, we must also actively participate in addressing the media with Christian information so as to take back the voice we have lost over these decades to more actively vocal liberal agencies.

Pray for Those Who Influence Your Children

Twenty years ago, LeeAnn and her late husband, Willard, had the opportunity as young parents to have dinner with Joyce Landorf, a well-known Christian speaker. At dinner, LeeAnn asked Joyce, "What can we do to help our boys grow up to be godly young men?"

"I believe that it's just as important to pray for our children's friends as it is to pray for our own children," Joyce replied.

"Is there anything we should specifically pray for them?" LeeAnn asked.

Joyce thought for a minute, then answered, "Well, I pray that God will bring friends into our children's lives. Friends who will be helpful. Friends who will be a good influence on them, and vice versa."

LeeAnn put Joyce's advice into practice, and through the years her boys have reaped the benefits of those prayers. They all have strong, godly friendships that developed in their younger years and grew deeper as they grew older. LeeAnn also found herself praying for her sons' various girlfriends, and over time, she prayed for three wonderful young women who became her daughters-in-law.

Friendships greatly influence a child's life, but there are other influences that we would also remember in prayer. We should pray for our children's grandparents, schoolteachers, Sunday school teachers, coaches and any neighbors they admire, to mention a few. Since these individuals can all make a difference in our children's lives, we need to pray that God will nurture the good in these relationships and make them as fruitful as they can possibly be.

Pray that God Will Nurture Their Vision and Protect Their Destiny

Make no small plans, for they have no ability to stir men's hearts.

I'm not sure where I read this quote, but it has stuck with me over the years. As we pray for our chil dren, it's important to ask God in faith for big dreams and a large vision for them, perhaps a vision that without His help would be impossible to accomplish.

In a world full of purposeless living that so easily slides into rebellion, we need to ask God to give our children a sense of purpose for their lives. We need to claim the righteous and godly goals He has for them. Of course, Satan loves nothing better than for our children to live a meaningless, purposeless existence, accomplishing little, if anything, for God's Kingdom. As a result, he will try energetically to draw them away from any vision and sense of destiny they may have for their lives. Paul told us in Ephesians 6:12:

> *For our struggle is not against flesh and blood, but against the rulers, against the authorities, against the powers of this dark world and against the spiritual forces of evil in the heavenly realms.*

The Bible tells us that Satan comes to rob, kill and destroy. Thus, we need to be constantly on guard so that he is unable to destroy our children and their future. As our children begin to move into God's destiny for them, Satan will place roadblocks in their way at every turn. We must prayerfully resist these unseen forces in Jesus' name.

One of the key places Satan attacks our children is in the talent or ability God has given them. He often uses people who unwittingly speak words of negativity or ridicule about our child's gifts.

Many thousands of young people today have been dissuaded from the high call God has for them by careless and thoughtless words. As parents, we need to be sure that we pray for wisdom in handling our children so as not to discourage the tiny seeds of faith and vision planted in their hearts.

Be a Model

We can very easily say as we tuck our children into bed, "Don't forget to say your prayers." But how will they know how to petition God unless we first and continually model for them how to pray?

Not long ago, LeeAnn was reflecting on a childhood prayer she, along with many other children, had learned: "God is great, God is good, and we thank Him for our food." A new realization hit her: What power there was in this simple prayer! A fellow YWAMer asked his little boy to pray for his sick mother. In all seriousness, the youngster touched her brow and recited the best prayer he knew, "God bless this food." The mother got well! It was not the language but the boy's sincerity that counted. We must help our children to see the truth related in simple prayers. God truly is great and good. If we can teach them to really believe in what their prayers convey, their concept of God would improve greatly.

If we kneel with our child beside his or her bed and pray, we model the importance of interceding for others as well as how to present our personal petitions to the Lord, engage in spiritual warfare and praise and thank God for all He does for us. Our children become effective prayer warriors by watching us and by participating with us in prayer. As they follow our model, our children are led into a wonderful devotional life of prayer. They come to recognize the value and importance of prayer. We can teach our children no greater lesson than prayer is the air that fills the believer's spiritual lungs.

Consider Fasting Along with Prayer

Some people may question the advisability of fasting by children or teenagers, but if done in moderation, fasting can be a valuable exercise in helping our children draw closer to God. Fasting can help them concentrate on His guidance for them as individuals as well as for the whole family. Matthew 6:16-18 reminds us not to make a big show of fasting, but to do it quietly, in secret, and God who sees in secret will reward us openly.

It is important to take the time to explain to our children exactly why we fast. Fasting is a discipline that most people will agree has both physical and spiritual advantages. Properly done, fasting helps cleanse the body of certain toxic materials, which helps us focus on certain issues as we pray. Such issues can include seeking the Lord's protection, receiving direction and leading from the Lord, expressing sorrow for our sins and adding authority to our prayers. We believe that short one- to three-day fasts can bring health and wholeness to a family. A strong key to healthy fasting is to drink a lot of fluids, which increases the body's ability to slough off impurities.

If you have never tried a simple fast, why not try it? Remember, our children learn best from example. Begin with a one-day fast. Get a good book on fasting so that the entire family is well informed, and fast as a team. Like many new and different activities, there is much to be learned and gained from this experience.

For our children to misinterpret fasting as "depriving oneself to win God's approval" is counterproductive. Over time, such misunderstanding may lead our children into thinking of God as someone who wants to take from them and make them miserable, when in fact the very opposite is true. If practiced carefully and wisely, family fasting can be a powerful tool in developing our children's relationship with the Lord.

Record Your Prayers

One of the most practical ways to increase our faith is to write down what we petition the Lord for on behalf of our children, and then to record the ways in which He answers those prayers. LeeAnn and I write our prayers, prayer requests and prayer lists in our prayer journal every day to help us keep on track with our praying. We record specific prayers with clear objectives.

LeeAnn and I both feel that recording what we pray is very important. Over the past fourteen years, I have accumulated forty prayer journals. Every so often, the Lord draws us back to those journals, and as we read them, we are humbled by the many ways in which He has answered our prayers.

Some people like to use a three-ring binder or a folder, keeping a section for each child. Others prefer to use a commercially produced prayer diary. Most importantly, whatever method we use preserves the requests we make to God, as well as the answers and insights He gives us for our children.

Encouraging our children to keep their own prayer journal is also a good idea. Over time, they can go back to their prayer log to see whether any patterns occur about things they pray over or insights God has given them during prayer. Such patterns can help them to understand more about themselves and the destiny God has for their lives.

Listen to God

Recently, our four-year-old granddaughter Alisha asked LeeAnn why my daughter and son-in-law were moving from Palm Springs to Colorado. LeeAnn explained that Mindy and Marty prayed and felt that God had told them to go to Colorado to participate in a church ministry team.

Alisha quickly replied, "Nannie, God doesn't talk to people."

"Yes He does, honey," LeeAnn told her. "But often we are too busy to hear His voice, because most of the time He speaks to our hearts and not to our ears."

Alisha was silent for a moment, and then she said, half to herself, "Hmmmm—must be too noisy at my house."

Truth from the mouths of babes! Sometimes our home can become so busy that those of us in it can't hear God's voice. If we can't, how can we expect our children to hear His voice? If too much frantic activity distracts us from taking time to be with God in prayer and listening for His voice, we need to slow down so we can hear what He is saying to us. We need to model to our children not only how to pray but also how to listen and to hear the voice of God.

Releasing Our Children

*The best thing about the
future is that it comes only
one day at a time.*
Abraham Lincoln

CHAPTER SEVEN

*W*e have a funny human trait whereby we spend most of our adult lives preparing our children to grow up and become independent and then, when they finally reach that point, we don't want to let them go!

LeeAnn found this to be true. She had so much fun being mother to three sons, but she knew she would be challenged to let her boys go as they grew up. The challenge was made a hundred times more difficult by the sudden death of her husband, Willard, from an aneurysm. Willard's death caused LeeAnn to hold on too tightly to her sons.

Six months after Willard died, their oldest son, Mark, and his wife, Laurie, set off to do a Discipleship Training School in New Zealand. Although LeeAnn missed them, she was grateful that at least they were in a safe place like New Zealand and not in some volatile Third-World country.

That is until she got a phone call from Mark After

some chitchat, he dropped the bombshell: "Mom, Laurie and I feel God is calling us to do our eight-week outreach in the Philippines."

LeeAnn's heart sank. The Philippines was in political turmoil. Her heart yelled, "No, no, no!" But she finally managed to say, "Oh, dear, are you sure? I sure don't hear anything like that."

LeeAnn had promised to help them financially with the outreach, but did God really expect her to help send them to such a dangerous place as the Philippines? Surely not!

LeeAnn agonized over the phone call. If only Willard were with her, he could reassure her that the kids were doing the right thing. But he wasn't, and LeeAnn was unsure of what to do.

Later that evening, LeeAnn's sister called and invited her to take part in her first grandson's dedication. That Sunday, as the pastor held the baby in his arms, he looked at the child and said, "You know, when our kids are small like this and we hold them in our arms and willingly give them to the Lord, we say, 'Lord, wherever; Timbuktu, it doesn't matter. They're Yours.' Then they grow up and are called to Timbuktu, and we say, 'No way!'"

LeeAnn recognized those words as God's words to her. God was challenging her. She felt His loving arms around her. LeeAnn had been angry with God, feeling that He could not possibly expect her to agree to His decision to send her son and daughter-in-law to the Philippines.

Then it hit her. Her mind went back 22 years to when she and Willard had stood together at the front of their church and dedicated Mark to the Lord.

Peace flooded her. She realized that the best and safest place for Mark was for him to be in God's will. She realized that she and Willard had already helped Mark make that decision many years before when they dedicated him to God's care.

As soon as LeeAnn got home, she phoned Mark and Laurie in New Zealand to give them her blessing on their outreach to the Philippines. She told Mark she'd found peace of mind, and that she would put a check in the mail the next day. But God was a step ahead of her. He had already supplied all the money Mark and Laurie needed for their trip! Despite LeeAnn's struggles to release Mark and Laurie to God's will, the Lord had already proved His faithfulness to them. The Lord didn't want LeeAnn's money; He just wanted a willing heart that would let go and release her son and his wife to Him. The financial provision was a wonderful confirmation that the Philippines was where the Lord wanted Mark and Laurie to go for their outreach.

When we dedicate our children as babies to the Lord, I doubt whether we realize the seriousness of our commitment. But as the years go by, God will test our resolve to be faithful to the commitment and to release our children into His hands. Several lines from the Gloria Gaither song, "I Wish You" sum up this experience perfectly:

We would like to collect you
And shield and protect you
And save you from hurts if we could.
But we must let you grow tall, to know all
That God has in mind for your good.
We never could own you,

For God only loaned you
To widen our world and our hearts.
So we wish you His freedom
Knowing where He is leading
There is nothing can tear us apart.

Our natural instinct is to shield our children from life's difficulties and hardships. But we can't. The cycle of life that God has set in place to rule His world necessitates that we release our children, no matter how rough the tempest of life around us might seem. Our turn has come to release our children and trust that what we built into their lives by our guidance and care throughout their growing years will allow them to steer a steady course through life.

When we release our children, we don't sever the parent-child relationship, we help it evolve. The relationship moves beyond our being directly responsible for our children. The child takes ownership of his or her own life, and we move into the role of life consultant.

Tragically, many parents don't make this transformation in their relationship. They try to hold on to their children, forcing their opinions and involving themselves in situations in their children's lives that they no longer have a right to be involved in. The irony is that rather than preserve the parent-child relationship, such actions only serve to alienate our children, forcing them away from us. More tragically, such actions often push children away from walking in and fulfilling the destiny God has for their life.

But as Christian parents, we want our children to grow up to love and serve God and fulfill the vision He has for their life. The best way to encourage that is by releasing our children to the Lord, by praying regularly for them, by being their consultant on life and by cheering and encouraging them.

Navigating Life

Navigating an ocean provides a good metaphor for living life. The ocean is constantly moving, constantly changing. Violent storms erupt and subside. The wind whips the surface of the water into foaming, surging mountains of waves and then, as quickly, returns the surface to polished glass. The ocean has many changing moods. So does life. Life can be calm and full of joy or filled with hardships and heartaches. It can be beautiful, and it can be ugly. It can be easy or hard, uplifting or bruising. Our lives are lived navigating these emotional currents, avoiding the treacherous reefs that threaten to shipwreck us. Just as we have made the journey, and our fathers before us, so must our children navigate life's currents, independent of us and on their own terms.

In her book *What Is Life?*, Catherine Casey sheds more light on the various facets of this journey of life we all take:

Life is a challenge...meet it.
Life is a journey...complete it.
Life is a struggle...fight it.
Life is a goal...achieve it.
Life is a beauty...praise it.
Life is a sorrow...overcome it.
Life is a tragedy...face it.
Life is a duty...perform it.
Life is a mystery...unfold it.
Life is a promise...fulfill it.

Duane Rawlins

Life is a song...sing it.
Life is an adventure...live it.
Life is a love...love it.

Our children will face many challenges as they step out on their own. If we try to shield them from life's difficulties, we only make it harder for them to face life head-on as eventually they must. As our children navigate life, they will face troubles, and they will make mistakes.

No one wants to make mistakes, or to see those they love make mistakes. But realistically, nothing teaches like experience. As we look back, we can see that we learned most things through experience— often negative experience through our own neglect, carelessness, or outright rebellion and disobedience. But we learned, no matter how painful the circumstance. And the next time a similar situation confronted us, we didn't make the same mistake.

So we must release our children to life's experiences. While we cannot shield them from these experiences, we can release our children to the Lord and trust that He will lead, guide and protect them. Thus, even after our children leave home and have families of their own, we need to continue to pray daily for them and hold them before the Lord. Our prayers need to be centered on asking the Lord to give them wisdom and strength in every area of life and, perhaps more importantly, to continue to nurture their vision until it comes to pass.

As our children move out from under our direct care, many things occur in life that threaten to choke their vision. Satan loves nothing better than to derail not only their vision but also their entire Christian

128

life by obvious lusts and temptations. Then there are the more subtle persuasions, such as career, money, family and friends. It is amazing how many people are hooked by their jobs, never moving into and fulfilling God's vision for their lives. Their job supplants their vision. Many others never fulfill their vision because of the debt they accumulate in amassing the trappings of the average American family.

Debt is a vision killer. Debt locks enthusiastic young people with vision into a buy-now-pay-later mentality. These people are trapped in a fruitless daily existence of just trying to pay for what they've already bought and grown tired of.

Family and friends can hold back still more people from grasping God's vision for them. Our spouse and our friends profoundly affect us, influencing the way we think and behave. If our child has a spouse or friends who are not sensitive to his or her vision, that vision can easily be stifled.

Being a Consultant

When our children become independent and leave home, our relationship with them changes. We no longer directly oversee their lives. We must release them to their own experiences in life and not step in unasked to solve their problems. Even when we are asked to help, it may not be advisable for us to do so, because the lessons our children learn from experience may be infinitely more valuable to them than our stepping in to solve the problem. God uses life's situations to teach and train us all. Therefore, we need to exercise great wisdom in handling our children's problems lest we circumvent God's purposes for our children in a situation.

Our role changes to one of consultant to our children after they leave home, rather than being an active problem solver for them. We can teach them tools on how to solve problems. We can share with our children six steps to effective problem solving:

Step 1. Identify and define the problem.
Step 2. Generate possible alternative solutions.
Step 3. Look carefully at and evaluate the alternatives.
Step 4. Mutually decide on the best solution.
Step 5. Work out ways to implement the solution.
Step 6. Follow up or evaluate how a solution worked.

When our children face a difficult situation or problem, we can make ourselves available for consultation. Drawing from our life experience and from our experience with the Lord, we can suggest ways to help them solve a problem or deal with a particular situation. We can offer a different perspective, seeing things perhaps our child cannot see, and advise him or her accordingly. Our motivation is not to solve the child's problem outright but to simply provide him or her with enough information for effective decision-making.

Consultants give their opinion about a situation, but don't decide on a solution. In the role of consultant, we may share our wisdom and counsel, but we must leave the problem where it belongs—with the child. And if the child decides on a different solution than ours, then he or she must shoulder the consequences of that decision.

Making Wise Choices

Offering our grown children suggestions for effectively solving problems and dealing with situations is not the only way we can consult. We can offer them our wisdom and insight on the many important decisions that they must make in life.

One of the early decisions our children may make is choosing a spouse. We can advise them on how to choose wisely, and can point out that they need to first seek God's will and approval. Our advice should be that they take their time and not rush into marriage. They should observe their potential spouse in a number of social settings, watching how he or she relates to and interacts with others.

Since so many things war against the success of marriages today, we must be sure to advise our children of the importance of their finding a Christian spouse who shares their view on major scriptural doctrines. The more of the basics of faith they agree upon, the fewer hassles they will have later over the practice of their faith. And as previously mentioned, the person our child marries can be a crucial factor in encouraging or deterring him or her from fulfilling his or her destiny. That is why the Bible teaches that we should not be unequally yoked with unbelievers. Too many young married people today are frustrated because they have had to lay down their calling to keep their marriage intact. By giving wise consultation, we can help keep our children from this pitfall.

Another consulting area is finances. Let's hope that we have instilled in our children solid financial principles so they know how to use money wisely. But they will have many financial decisions to make after they leave home, such as buying a home of their own, purchasing a car and obtaining insurance, not to mention saving and investing money. Most of us will have had some experience with such decisions and can offer helpful advice. We also need to focus on helping our children establish a financial base from which they can step out to fulfill the destiny and call God has for their life. Of course, God may call them to step out completely in faith, and if that is the case, we should encourage and support them. But it is a matter of good stewardship to work to establish a stable financial base from which to launch out into serving God, and we must encourage our children accordingly.

Our job should also involve helping our children keep their eyes on the vision God has given them. If we do this, our children are less likely to be ensnared by the subtle hooks of materialism. We should remind our children of Deuteronomy 8:18: "But remember the Lord your God, for it is he who gives you the ability to produce wealth, and so confirms his covenant." Anyone wanting to pursue his or her destiny in God should have that perspective. God gives us the power to create or earn wealth, and He does it to confirm His covenant to us. If our children become wise stewards of the wealth the Lord gives them, when He calls them to service, they will be able to say like Isaiah of old, "Here am I, Lord, send me," and not, "Here am I, Lord. When I've paid off these credit cards, I'll be right with You."

God may ask us to invest our resources to help our children fulfill their vision. We should be prepared to do so. However, we must be sure that we give to our children according to God's will and not just because we feel sorry for them or don't want to see them go without. If we give for those reasons, we can easily undermine God's teaching in their life. So give according to God's leading, and if He tells you to invest in their life and vision, invest generously to encourage their service for the Lord.

Remember also, consultants and advisers wait to be asked to become involved in a situation, they don't force their way in.

Releasing Versus Abandoning

Families are forever. We are not required to abandon our children to life's currents as they grow up, but we are asked to release them. There will always be a place in our heart and our home for our grown children, their children and their children's children.

Our children need to know that if they hurt, if they fail, if they suffer bitter disappointment, then like the father in the parable of the prodigal son, we are there for them when they return home. Home is the place where they can find forgiveness, acceptance, love and healing, a place where they don't have to feel defeated or ashamed.

If we release our children and make the transition this release needs, we will never lose them. The bonds of our relationship with them—while different than they used to be—will be deeper and stronger, lasting into eternity.

Beyond Parenting

*It is high time the ideal of success
should be replaced
by the ideal of service.*

Albert Einstein

CHAPTER EIGHT

*P*erhaps you find yourself in a similar situation to ours: free of the daily demands of our own children but still having parenting skills to offer. The great news is that just because our children grow up and leave home doesn't mean there is nothing left for us to do. Quite the opposite. Many opportunities exist where our experience can be greatly utilized.

God is the ultimate recycler! He looks at our mistakes, our successes, our insights picked up over a lifetime of raising our children, and He says, "I can use those things in My kingdom." He is not finished with us yet. If we live a life of submission to Jesus Christ, everything we experience has a purpose for His kingdom, and that purpose doesn't end when our children leave home.

Beyond parenting, we can put our nurturing instincts to work by becoming effective grandparents to our children's children. We can also mentor other people's children. In addition, we can reparent adults who grew up with a severe lack of parental nurturing and guidance.

All who find themselves at a station in life similar to LeeAnn's and mine have plenty within these three categories to keep themselves busy and their parenting skills well-honed.

Grandparenting: A Joy and a Privilege

Being a grandparent is like watching from the balcony. We don't have direct responsibility for our grandchildren, so we stand back and cheer them on. Grandparents are those who can say, "You can do it." "I'm proud of you." "I have confidence in you." "Go ahead and try." "So what if you fail. We all fail sometimes. The important thing is to try."

Children need someone to believe in and encourage them, and as their grandparents, we can do precisely that. We can be cheerleaders for our grandchildren, helping them feel good about themselves and the way God designed them.

This role becomes even more important in the busy, pressure-filled world in which our children live. Often such busyness and pressure mean that our sons and daughters and their spouses are working. As grandparents, we can step in and help fill the gap in our grandchildren's lives to give them the special individual attention they need to thrive.

Time is one of the greatest gifts we have to offer to anyone, and we can give our time by talking and listening to our grandchildren. Talking to our grandchildren can have a tremendous impact on their lives. If we were to sit down and talk with our grandchild for ten minutes every time we met, we would have a greater impact on the child's thinking than if the child were to spend an hour studying each day. That ten minutes could be the highlight of our grandchild's day. All we have to do is find something the child is interested in and ask him or her about it.

When we ask questions of a person, we validate that person. We force the person to collect his or her thoughts, put them into words and speak them. Especially with children, answering questions about their interests becomes a challenging and growing experience. Be ready for silence, however, when you ask a young child a question. It takes at least twenty seconds for a child to process a question and come up with an answer. Ask the question and then enjoy the silence as the child thinks about what you've asked.

Given our busy lives, special times alone with our grandchildren are unlikely to happen unless we carefully plan for them and make them a priority. We have thirteen grandchildren. Although finding time to spend with each one is hard, we decided a year or so ago to take each one out for his or her birthday to a nice dinner or to the place of his or her choice. This gives us quality time with each child. We share a special memory of one of our granddaughters saying to us after her fourth-birthday dinner, "Nannie and Poppie, I will never forget this place." Little things mean so much to small children. Be creative and do special things that bless your grandchildren.

After my son Mark died from cancer, my daughter-in-law Lynne and her four children moved to Salem to be closer to the rest of the family. Since my three grandsons and my granddaughter now have no dad, I feel a special burden to give as much support

to them as I possibly can. I make sure we do things together.

I recently took my five-year-old grandson out to eat for a special birthday lunch, just the two of us. I let him order whatever he liked. I'm sure it wasn't a very healthful lunch: a corn dog, French fries, a cola, and a hot fudge sundae. But I knew that it was special to him because of the wonderful hug and kiss he gave me afterward.

By spending time with each grandchild, I have another aim. Mark was a vibrant Christian who spent much of his adult life on the mission field. My hope is that through getting to know their granddad, Mark's children will catch some of the vision their father had for serving the Lord. As I spend time with his children, I'm able to talk about how their dad loved the Lord, and about the things he used to do.

Grandparents often have more time to organize the "extra" things that will live forever in a child's memory. This past Christmas, LeeAnn and I took some of our grandchildren to a nursing home to sing Christmas songs. Before going, we practiced a few carols, and even though we didn't sound too professional, we sang the songs cheerfully. I'm not sure who was more blessed, the elderly people we visited or LeeAnn and I. This special occasion truly made that Christmas a wonderful memory for all of us.

We encourage you to take advantage of the many opportunities you have for becoming involved in the lives of your grandchildren. There are so many creative ways to do this. Be a blessing to your grandchildren, and be blessed in the process.

Mentoring Other People's Children

Once you have finished parenting your own children, you can become involved in the lives of other young people in a number of ways. There are young people who desperately need positive role models from older, wiser people who they know will care about them and their problems.

As our culture deteriorates, we find more and more of these needy children in church youth groups and in community programs such as Boy Scouts, Girl Scouts, Indian Guides and the YMCA. These young people may spend their time aimlessly wandering the streets or spend countless hours in video arcades. They may be children who are coping with a parent's dying from AIDS, children who need a friend and advocate as they go through complicated legal procedures, or children who need to adjust to temporary foster homes or newly adoptive families. Everywhere we turn, we see young people crying out for love, encouragement and attention.

James 1:27 tells us: "Religion that God our Father accepts as pure and faultless is this: to look after orphans and widows in their distress and to keep oneself from being polluted by the world." Within each of our extended families and circle of friends and acquaintances are bound to be children who need extra adult support. These children can give us an opportunity to practice James's injunction. Many of them need to experience firsthand the pure and faultless love of God.

Since the death of my oldest son, my daughter and son-in-law have stepped in to try to fill a small part of the gap Mark left. Even though they live several states away, Marty and Mindy make sure they see their niece and nephews at least a couple of times a year, and they keep track by telephone of how the children are doing. My son Matthew and his wife, Celia, live close to the children, and are always looking for creative ways to help and love the kids. The little things Matt does with them doesn't completely remove the deep hurts that accompany the loss of their father, but they help.

Children feel their parents have to be interested in what they do and who they are, but when other adults—who don't have to be interested in them—make time for them, it boosts their self-esteem.

No matter how you become involved in mentoring other people's children, the most important thing is to stay committed. Once a child expects that you will be there to help, he or she could be devastated to find out that you weren't really that committed after all. The old saying, "God prizes availability over ability," holds particularly true when mentoring. Our being there for a child, our praying for the child and our commitment to the child's welfare speak much louder to the child than an eloquent lecture.

Indirect Ways to Mentor Other People's Children

> *You must teach what is in accord with sound doctrine. Teach the older men to be temperate, worthy of respect, self-controlled, and sound in faith, in love and in endurance. Likewise, teach the older women to be reverent in the way they live, not to be slanderers or addicted to much wine, but to*

> *teach what is good. Then they can train the*
> *younger women to love their husbands and*
> *children, to be self-controlled and pure, to*
> *be busy at home, to be kind, and to be sub-*
> *ject to their husbands, so that no one will*
> *malign the word of God.* —Titus 2:1-5

A few years ago, as LeeAnn was riding along the freeway with a younger friend, her friend looked over at her and said, "My husband and I just love watching you and Willard together. It helps us learn ways to love each other. You know, I think older women need to teach us younger women how to love our husbands." That conversation became one of the seeds for LeeAnn's first book, *Loving Your Husband for Life.*

The wisdom of the apostle Paul's words to Titus are obvious. What better way to learn how to be a good parent than to observe a good parent at work? There are so many areas of life in addition to parenting where older men and women can mentor younger men and women. All it takes is an older person willing to mentor and a younger person willing to learn.

Although there are many levels at which we can affect other people's children, one of the most effective and simplest things we can do is to pray for them. Until we get to heaven, we will never fully realize the impact our prayer has on these children or their families.

LeeAnn remembers an old prayer warrior who spent hours each day praying. One Sunday morning after church, this woman told LeeAnn, "Every Monday morning when your son Lonnie sets off for a new week of school, I pray for him." What a blessing for

LeeAnn and Willard to know that their son was being covered by extra prayer every week. Be a prayer warrior. Ask God to give you other people's children to pray for. The rewards are great for you and the child, as well as for the child's parents.

One of my first jobs was cleaning rugs. I worked with the company owner in the basement of his business establishment before school. Every morning before he began his tasks, he would ask me to join him in prayer for our work together and for the rest of the day. His actions had a profound impact on me as I sensed the closeness of his relationship with the Lord.

We can have a similar impact on the lives of the young people around us. We can mentor them, pray for them, share the love of God borne in their hearts. We can inspire them to grow up to love and serve God. All it takes is a willing and committed heart on our part.

Reparenting Others

A young girl who came from a very difficult family situation lived with my first wife, Betty, and me for a period of time. She had been adopted by American missionaries, and after the mother died, the adoptive father began an incestuous relationship with the girl's sister. When this young girl moved in with us, she was full of emotional hurt, bitterness and rebellion. Having her live with us wasn't easy, and Betty and I learned many things as we went along. But we didn't give up. We kept loving her and praying for her. As she struggled with the swirl of emotions she was feeling, we talked and listened and kept praying for her and loving her. We tried to make up for the deficit she had experienced from her own parents. Eventually, we were able to help her get her life back on track. Today, that young woman serves the Lord as a missionary, and she has a wonderful husband and family of her own.

Our deteriorating society has created not only a whole category of children who need the input of adults, but it has also created a similar category of adults. These are people who grew up in homes where they were not loved and nurtured, where they were violated and abused—both physically and emotionally—and who may have been kicked out of the home when they were teenagers. These people need to be reparented. They need a loving, nurturing, and physically and emotionally safe place where the scars of the past can heal. They need a place where they can experience the emotional and practical input of loving surrogate parents. They need a place where they can grow and learn the skills necessary to successfully handle life. They need a place where they can experience the love and acceptance of God.

Some years after our experience with the missionaries' adopted daughter, LeeAnn and I invited a young pregnant woman to stay in our home. This young woman had decided to have her child adopted into a Christian home. We were able to walk through the whole ordeal with her. We witnessed the tremendous psychological pain she went through in giving up her child for adoption. We tried to comfort and support her as best we could. She progressed in her walk with the Lord, and eventually she married a fine Christian man. It is a delight today to see her wholeness and the way she is striving to live for Christ.

It's not always easy to become involved with peo،

ple in need. It takes a lot of patience and emotional energy. But it is so rewarding to see the personal growth that takes place when people are loved and accepted for who they are. Their whole countenance changes when they know someone believes in them and wants to help them.

Of course, Satan likes nothing better than to immobilize our efforts by telling us that we should be perfect at something before we attempt it! We are foolish if we buy his line. We are all people in process. The people we reach out to are in process. Our children are in process. Our grandchildren are in process. We should go easy on ourselves and fight the urge to be perfect before taking on a task of such importance. The need is too great to wait for perfection!

Right now, hundreds of thousands of children in the United States have no idea what a stable marriage looks like. They don't often see marital stability in their own home or in their friends' homes, and they certainly don't often see it portrayed in the media. If any of these young people came into our home and observed as we did nothing more than be ourselves and relate to others in a godly fashion, it would completely boggle such a child's mind and challenge his or her thinking!

Satan likes to constantly remind us of our past failures. When he does, we can tell him that mistakes are to be learned from. All our favorite Bible characters made mistakes—some of them even with child-raising! For example, Eli's own sons were an abysmal failure, yet God entrusted Eli with the task of raising Samuel. Even if you failed at child raising in the past, don't write yourself off—God doesn't.

And yes, it's okay to be tired. It's okay to feel frustrated. We're not super-humans. We have limitations, and it's good to recognize them lest Satan tries to condemn and defeat us because of them.

Parenting is about nurturing a person's vision, dreams, strengths and relationships. If we learn to nurture in this way, we will create the best possible environment for that person to blossom into everything God has prepared for him or her.

In her book, *Nobody's Children,* Valerie Bell calls nurturers compassionate, even-tempered, understanding, good-humored, trustworthy and affectionate. She claims that nurturers practice a lifestyle of noncompetitiveness, maintain a sense of wonder and awe toward life and, most importantly, value life and believe in God.

We must understand that, as Bell says, in raising our children, we are "cooperating in a holy venture." We are "chosen and strategically placed by God to minister His love unreservedly...." Most importantly, we are called to raise godly children who will carry on this great joy and privilege for generations to come.

Children are God's greatest gift to parents. And parents are God's greatest gift to children. What a divinely orchestrated exchange!

Additional Books by the Rawlins

- *Loving Your Husband for Life* by LeeAnn Rawlins
- *More Than a Father* by Duane Rawlins

Any of these books are available through:

New Life Ministries
7085 Battlecreek Road S.E.
Salem, Oregon 97301
                or
Emerald Books
P.O. Box 635
Lynnwood, Washington 98046

If you would like to write to us about any of our books, or just for love and encouragement as you parent, please do. Write to us at:

Dr. and Mrs. Duane Rawlins
7085 Battlecreek Road S.E.
Salem, Oregon 97301